OLYMPIANS IN VACATIONLAND

The Legendary Training Camp at Bowdoin College
And the Athletes who took on the World in Munich

D. Todd Coffin

ISBN:
979-8-9865517-0-8 – Linen Hardcover
979-8-9865517-1-5 – Case Laminate Hardcover
979-8-9865517-2-2 – Paperback
979-8-9865517-3-9 – Digital EBook

v2022.08.23

OLYMPIANS IN VACATIONLAND

Is Dedicated to:

Frank Sabasteanski
Head Coach, Bowdoin College Track and Field (1955-1983)

Walter Slovenski
Head Coach, Bates College Track and Field (1952-1996)

Jim Wescott
Head Coach, Colby College Track and Field (1978-2003)

You improved countless lives as coaches, mentors and friends.

Acknowledgments

Project 72 would not have been possible without a dedicated team that provided support, ideas, and invaluable feedback. I wish to extend heartfelt gratitude to Dr. Herbert T. Caverly, II, and his son, Bud, for those dusty photos that started Project 72 off the blocks; to Steve Podgajny and Doug Morrell, whose knowledge, passion and drive helped immensely through every lap; to Dave Wottle, Jeff Galloway, Jan Johnson and Fred Luke for sharing so much of their time and lending encouragement in the late miles; and to Max, Alex and Lorena, whose love, guidance, and encouragement brought Project 72 across the line.

Special thanks to the professional partners of Project 72: Mark Coffin, Seyfarth Shaw LLP; Justin Tafoya, Clarkson Creative Photography; and Blaine Moore, Midcoast Publishing. Your guidance and enthusiasm helped bring *Olympians in Vacationland* to light.

Table of Contents

Olympic javelin qualifier Fred Luke in a work-out session at Whittier Field. (Author's personal collection)

Preface

IN 1991, MY WIFE AND I WERE CLEARING A BOOKSHELF IN her family home in Bath, Maine, when I came across a small cardboard box. I lifted the dusty lid and saw it contained a stack of glossy black and white photo enlargements. The images were athletes training at a place I knew well—Whittier Field at Bowdoin College. I had trained and raced on the red tartan track where these men—some powerful, some sleek—had assembled. Many of the photos were signed: *Jeff Galloway, Rod Milburn, Jack Bacheler, Lee Evans, Preston Carrington and Steve Prefontaine.* My heart raced because I knew I was holding something special.

The photos belonged to my brother-in-law, Bud Caverly, who remembered that in 1972, the US men's track and field Olympic team attended a ten-day training camp at Bowdoin College before departing for the Olympics in Munich. Bud explained that shortly after the training camp, a local photographer gave the photo collection to his dad, Herbert Caverly, a Bowdoin graduate and local dentist. Neither Bud nor his dad could recall the name of the photographer. A week later, I stopped by my in-laws and noticed a familiar cardboard box sitting on the kitchen table. A sticky note read, "Please take these. I know you'll appreciate them more than I ever will—Bud."

I transferred the photos into an album and stowed the collection, for a second time, on a bookshelf. Years later, I showed the photo collection to Steve Podgajny, a fellow marathoner and director of the Curtis Memorial Library in Brunswick, Maine. After thumbing through the stack, he said, "You know, Todd, I know a guy who has some pictures you need to see."

The guy was Doug Morrell, whose father Bob owned a cottage in nearby Mere Point. In 1972, Bob volunteered to host a lobster bake for about two dozen of the track and field Olympians. Doug shared a set of black and white Polaroids and 35 mm color photos taken at the lobster bake and at the Whittier Field track. Doug's photographs added an intimate perspective of the Olympians' stay in Maine, and I realized that the growing photo collection provided the foundation for a retrospective of the historic event—*Olympians in Vacationland.*

At the lobster bake with host family members Doug Morrell (far left) and his mother, Nan Morrell (far right) chatting with Steve Prefontaine. (Courtesy of Doug Morrell)

Jan Wottle displays her lobster with host Bob Morrell looking on. (Courtesy of Dave Wottle)

I searched for more photos of the Olympians in Maine with outreach to area historical societies, college and high school alumni, running clubs, social media sites and contact with several of the '72 Olympians. The quest uncovered only five more photos. Dave Wottle, who competed in the 800 meters and 1,500 meters at the Munich Games, provided three photos taken at the lobster bake. Pole vaulter Jan Johnson shared a single snapshot of Steve Prefontaine he took during a walk through the Bowdoin College neighborhood.

The fifth photo was of Steve Prefontaine strolling shirtless down the Bowdoin College track. The photo appeared on a social media website with the username "Happy Rower." It turned out the Happy Rower was Scott Wilson, a Maine native and track coach whose father was a spectator at the training camp and had photographed the athletes. Scott told me he had last seen his dad's '72 photo collection in a shoe box, but the only image he could find was the one of Prefontaine.

The *Olympians in Vacationland* project languished for over a decade as leads dwindled and the quest for photos stalled. Then, in 2016, I learned that staff at the Portland Public Library, including archivist Abraham Schechter, helped rescue thousands of photo negatives from the basement of a building formerly occupied by Maine's largest newspaper, the *Portland Press Herald.* The building had been undergoing renovations, and the negatives were only days away from transport to a smelter. Once again, the trail led to Steve Podgajny, who had recently retired as director of the Portland Public Library. When Steve learned the photo negatives might include images from the '72 training camp, he reached out to Abraham. Within a few days, Abraham re-energized the project with three dozen trackside photos of the visiting Olympians captured by the *Press Herald's* sports photographers.

To date, I have discovered trackside photos of 35 Olympic athletes who came to Maine in July 1972. The athletes captured on film stirred research into the path that led each to the Olympics in Munich and their life's journey after 1972. Besides photos of the athletes in Maine, *Olympians in Vacationland* includes images of the athletes competing at the Munich Games and other

Steve Prefontaine at Whittier Field.
(Courtesy of Scott Wilson)

track and field venues. I interviewed several of the Olympians who trained in Maine, and their recollections added insight to their stay in Maine, including memorable quotes that are captured in the retrospective.

"The Whittier Field Sessions," the opening chapter of *Olympians in Vacationland,* includes biographical highlights of the 36 athletes photographed at Whittier Field. I discovered photos of pole vaulter Jan Johnson and high jumper Ron Jourdan only at the lobster bake, and the two Olympians are introduced in the respective photo captions. Among the athletes not identified in the *Olympians in Vacationland* photo collection were Munich medalists George Woods (silver, shot put); Jay Silvester (silver, discus); Dwight Stones (bronze, high jump); Bill Schmidt (bronze, javelin); Arnie Robinson (bronze, long jump); Thomas Hill (bronze, 110-meter hurdles); and Larry Young (bronze, 50-kilometer race walk). Team members who did not join the voluntary training camp included Wayne Collett (400 meters), Jim Ryun (1,500 meters), George Young (5,000 meters), Bob Seagren (pole vault), and John Craft (triple jump)—and possibly others among the 68 athletes who qualified for the Munich Olympics.

The gateway to Whittier Field stadium.
(Courtesy of Blaine Moore)

Welcome to Vacationland

ON JULY 19, 1972, 54 MEMBERS OF THE UNITED STATES Olympic Men's Track and Field team swept into the small coastal town of Brunswick, Maine.[1] The town is home to Bowdoin College, whose Whittier Field stadium was selected as the site of the training camp that would prepare the team for the Olympic Games in Munich. For ten days the team slept in Bowdoin's dorms, ate in the campus dining hall and honed their formidable skills on the tartan track and grass fields of the stadium. They were among the last true amateurs of their sport and the medal favorites included emerging distance icons Frank Shorter and Steve Prefontaine, sprinters Eddie Hart and Rey Robinson, hurdler Rod Milburn, and decathlete Jeff Bannister.

Bill Bowerman led the Olympians as the coach whose University of Oregon teams won four National Collegiate Athletic Association (NCAA) track titles and included 64 All-Americans, 33 Olympians, and 22 world-record holders. In the months preceding the camp, Bowerman and business partner Phil Knight had manufactured running shoes by a start-up company named after the Greek goddess of victory—Nike. A handful of distance runners cruised the winding coastal roads in newly minted Nike trainers, while members of the sprint team wore T-shirts embossed with the familiar Nike swoosh, launching one of the first marketing campaigns for the iconic brand.

Most of the athletes had never visited Maine, also known as Vacationland for its renowned lodges and summer camps nestled among pristine beaches, lakes, and mountains. The '72 Olympians were competitors forged from the track and field proving grounds of California and Oregon, two states that would host the Olympic Trials from 1952 to 1984. Their arrival in a state better known for fresh seafood than its track lore would have been inconceivable if not for the influence of three long-time Bowdoin College staff members with Olympic team ties—Dr. Dan Hanley, Chief Nurse Barbara Sabasteanski, and her husband, Coach Frank Sabasteanski.

Bowdoin College's Whittier Field stadium in 2018, site of the 1972 Olympic training camp. (Courtesy of Scott Hanson)

Bowdoin track coach and Olympic camp director, Frank Sabasteanski. (Copyright Bowdoin College)

Bowdoin's head physician from 1946 to 1980, Dr. Hanley became an assistant physician for the Olympic team in 1960 and was chief physician of the US Olympic team from 1964 through 1972. Barbara Sabasteanski served as an Olympic team nurse at the Tokyo Games in 1964, the Mexico City Games in 1968 and joined the team at the Olympics in Munich.

Frank Sabasteanski had been head coach of Bowdoin's track team since 1955 and rose to national prominence as a coach for US track and field athletes during pre-Olympic competition in Mexico City in 1965. He coached the US team that competed against Russia and the British Commonwealth in Los Angeles in 1969, and in 1971, was co-director of a summer training camp that brought 30 of the nation's top jumpers and vaulters to Bowdoin College.

Beyond Bowdoin's staff connections with the US Olympic team, Whittier Field boasted a world-class tartan track laid just a year earlier, and Maine's climate was like Munich's. The *Portland Press Herald* reported that one of the few complaints of the Olympic athletes was the lack of nightlife, and added, "...perhaps that was one reason for selecting Bowdoin and Brunswick as the training site."[2]

The serenity of Whittier Field, with its sentinel pines and sun-drenched bleachers, would stand in stark contrast with the turmoil and tragedy of the Munich Games less than a month away. Before the opening ceremony, Ethiopia, Kenya, Uganda and several black athletes on the US team threatened to boycott the Games because of the participation of Rhodesia, a country with overt racist policies. Under mounting international pressure, the International Olympic Committee (IOC) voted to expel Rhodesia, putting an end to the protests. IOC President Avery Brundage remarked, "The political pressures in sport are becoming intolerable."[3]

On September 5, two weeks into the Munich Games, eight Palestinian militants assaulted the Israeli team apartment complex, killing two athletes and taking nine hostages. The nine hostages were later killed during a failed rescue attempt by the West German government.

It was not clear if the Games would, or should, continue. In the wake of a monumental security collapse, many athletes felt vulnerable and were stunned by the horror that unfolded in the public eye. US Olympic marathoner Kenny Moore later wrote: "In that uncertainty, we experienced level after level of grief. I remember weeping for my own event, the marathon, for years of preparation that seemed wasted, and for the violated sanctuary of the Games."[4] Kenny Moore and Frank Shorter would run their event on the last day of the Games, placing first and fourth, the best marathon finish for the US team since the London Games in 1908.

Before the protest and senseless massacre, before Eddie Hart and Rey Robinson missed their qualifying 100-meter heats, and before an imposter ran onto the track during Frank Shorter's epic marathon finish, the Olympic trackmen prepared in the embrace of Maine's fans and sports media who treated them as heroes. They dined on succulent lobster, waterskied on chilly water, and greeted the daily throngs of onlookers with warm smiles and flowing autographs on hats, T-shirts and scraps of paper. Hundreds of cameras clicked, and video cameras whirled as the athletes tuned their starts, perfected their throws, and prepared for the world stage ahead.

On the morning of their tenth day in Maine, the US track and field athletes boarded a plane that would take them to pre-Olympic meets in Norway and, soon after, the Munich Games. Several would achieve Olympic glory, while others would falter and return home deeply disappointed. After the Games they would start families, earn doctorates, author autobiographies, advocate for civil rights and coach athletes who would themselves become Olympians.

The US Olympic team during the opening ceremony in Munich, August 26, 1972. (Rich Clarkson Collection)

Olympic 400-meter hurdle qualifier Richard Bruggeman at Whittier Field. (Courtesy of Portland Public Library Special Collections & Archives)

The Whittier Field Sessions

Fans watch from the curve during an Olympic team workout at Whittier Field. (Courtesy of Doug Morrell)

THE OLYMPIANS WHO GATHERED in Maine worked out twice a day to the delight of hundreds of spectators who descended on the athletes with autograph books, cameras, and awe-struck greetings. Admission was free, and fans spilled out of the stands and onto the track for an arm's length view of the athletes in action. Businesses in town hummed as stores sold out of film and lines swelled in the local restaurants. Commuters came upon the US distance squad training on town roads. "Marathoners took their lives in their running shoes to negotiate the narrow, winding coastal roads," commented Dick Dew of the *Boston Herald*. "It was not uncommon to see a lonely plodder braving traffic and the evening shower on the causeway to Bailey's Island, 15 miles from campus."[5]

The host venue, Whittier Field, was an athletic complex constructed in 1896 and named after Bowdoin College athletic director and physician Dr. Frank Nathanial Whittier. While renowned for its historic grandstand and towering pines, the facility was equipped with a new track and finely groomed fields for the throwing events. As reported by Dew, the caliber of the throwers prompted the only change to the venue: "Where the Bowdoin athletes had plenty of room, the cream of the US discuss, javelin and weight men were throwing the darned things clean over the fences, compelling a hasty relocation of the practice area."[5]

Before the end of the training camp, Olympic organizers provided the athletes with physicals, shots, team uniforms and passports. On July 28, the team boarded a bus to the Portland jetport and departed for New York City and connecting flights to Oslo, Norway for extended pre-Olympic training and competition. Harry Shulman of the *Portland Press Herald* wrote, "The squad has wound up a ten-day training period here, recording an exciting and historic chapter in Maine sports annals…Never have Maine natives and summer visitors been privileged to observe so many of this country's and the world's finest in action."[2]

Decathlete Jeff Bannister at the throwing circle, Whittier Field. (Author's personal collection)

Jeff Bannister

Jeff Bannister was raised in Scarborough, Maine, and his return to the Pine Tree State as a member of the Olympic track and field team in 1972 was celebrated by track fans and the press. Bannister was the top qualifier in the decathlon at the Olympic Trials in Eugene, Oregon, 44 points ahead of Jeff Bennett of the US Army. Bannister's marks at the Trials included 6 feet 6 inches (6-6) in the high jump, 24-1 in the long jump, and 47.7 seconds in the 400 meters. He was ranked No. 2 in the world leading up to the Munich Games.

Bannister was a standout in basketball and track at Cheverus High School in Portland, Maine, and following a post-graduate year at Worcester Academy, he competed in both sports at the University of New Hampshire. Bannister entered his first decathlon in 1967, inspired by fellow Worcester Academy alumn Bill Toomey, who won the decathlon at the Mexico City Games in 1968. Bannister placed third in the AAU decathlon championship in 1969, and improved to second at the championship in 1972, in a close finish with the winner, Jeff Bennett. One month later at the Trials, the top two spots would be reversed.

Jeff Bannister during an interview at Whittier Field. (Courtesy of Portland Public Library Special Collections & Archives)

Bannister told the Portland Press Herald *during an interview on July 23, 1972, "I don't feel you should wear national uniforms or play national anthems. The basis of the Olympics is non-political, and it makes me sad countries would use them for propaganda purposes."*[6]

At the Munich Games, the decathlon was scheduled to begin on September 6, but was postponed for the memorial service to honor the hostages killed during the terrorist attack the previous day. In an interview published by *The Boston Globe* on September 6, 1972, Bannister commented, "It's tough, because you have to sort of regroup yourself for the event coming a day later, but it's tough for everybody."[7]

After the first day of competition in the decathlon on September 7, Bannister was in 10th place with two of his strongest events scheduled for day two—the 110-meter hurdles and the 1,500 meters. But in the 110-meter hurdles, Bannister fell and was disqualified for failing to complete all the hurdle flights. Despite placing third in the 1,500 meters, the points he lost in the hurdles dropped Bannister to 21st in the final standings.

Around 1973, Bannister retired from competition and became Nike's 48th employee working out of the fledgling company's Eugene, Oregon headquarters. He left Nike to become general manager, and later Senior Vice President, for the watersports giant, O'Brien International in Redmond, Washington. Jeff retired as President of Connelly Skis, Inc., in 2016.

Jeff Bannister celebrates his high jump mark on the way to victory at the Olympic Trials in 1972. (Press photo)

Bannister qualified for the Munich Games by winning the 1972 Trials with a personal best of 8,120 points—a score that would have won silver in Munich.

Jeff Bennett

At just 5-8 and 152 pounds, Jeff Bennett defied the stature typical of decathletes whose events include the high hurdles, high jump, shot put, discus and javelin, among others. Yet, at the Olympic trials in 1972, Bennett avenged a fifth-place finish in the 1968 Olympic qualifier by finishing second to Jeff Bannister and securing a spot at the Games in Munich. On day two of decathlon competition at the Trials, he and Bannister had built such a comfortable lead that they ran side-by-side in the last event, the 1,500 meters.

A native of Vinita, Oklahoma, Bennet excelled in track in high school and college. He won the state pole vault championship as a high school senior, then claimed three national titles at Oklahoma Christian University: the 400-meter hurdles in 1968 and the decathlon in 1969 and 1970. While Bennett excelled in the hurdles and 400-meter dash, the pole vault was Bennett's first love and became his strongest event. In an interview with *The Joplin Globe* in 2016, Bennett recalled, "When I was about 8 years old, my friends and I set up a homemade pole vault pit in one of my friend's yard. We set 2x4s in the ground and hammered nails in them for the standards. We used a string with weights on each end for the crossbar and got an old antenna to use for the pole."[8]

Jeff Bennett on the backstretch at Whittier Field. (Courtesy of Portland Public Library Special Collections & Archives)

Nicknamed by sportswriters as the "Miniature Marvel" and "Little Bennett," Bennett excelled in the decathlon in Munich placing third in the 100 meters (10.73), second in the 400 meters (46.79), second in the 1,500 meters (4:12.2) and first in the pole vault (15-0 ¾). At the end of the two-day event, Bennett finished fourth with a score of 7,974, a scant ten points away from the bronze medal. Bennett later recalled, "I spent some sleepless nights at first, thinking where I could have made up 10 points? What if I had long jumped an inch farther? What if I had ran just a little faster? But I soon came to realize that it was just a tremendous experience to compete against the top athletes and finish fourth in the world."[8]

Bennett won the national AAU decathlon championship in 1973, setting a personal record of 8,121 points, but a hamstring injury kept him out of the Olympic Trials and a shot at the Montreal Games in 1976. Bennett returned to Oklahoma Christian University, where he served as Dean of Students and an assistant track coach.

Olympic decathlete Jeff Bennett with the javelin at Whittier Field. (Author's personal collection)

Jeff Bennett on the track infield at Bowdoin. (Author's personal collection)

Bennett's bald eagle "VOTE" T-shirt was among his favorites. "I was not interested in politics," he explained. "I liked the shirt because of the eagle. My college mascot was the eagle and as an army NCO, the eagle was also important."

Bruce Jenner

At the '72 Olympic Trials, it was clear coming into day two of the decathlon who the top two qualifiers were for the Munich Games—Jeff Bannister and Jeff Bennett. But the third spot on the team came down to the last event, the 1,500 meters. The last ticket to Munich was awarded to the winner of the 1,500 meters, a 22-year-old from Graceland College, Bruce Jenner. On July 5, 1972, the Eugene Register-Guard ran the headline: "Bannister, Bennett Make Team, But Who's Jenner?"[9]

Jenner at the training camp in Brunswick, Maine. (Courtesy of Portland Public Library Special Collections & Archives)

The Munich Games motivated Jenner to become the best in the world. In an interview with ESPN in 2015, Jenner commented that after finishing 10th, "I literally started training that night…running through the streets of Munich, Germany, training for the Games. I trained that day on through the 1976 Games, 6-8 hours a day, every day, 365 days a year."[10]

Jenner was born in Mount Kisco, New York, and attended schools in New York and Connecticut. Jenner was athletic at an early age and became accomplished in football, basketball, wrestling, track, and waterskiing. After a knee injury ended a promising first-year football season at Graceland College, Jenner focused on track and field. J. D. Weldon, the coach who lured Jenner to Graceland with a $500 annual scholarship, convinced his recruit to try the decathlon.[11] In the spring of 1970, Jenner placed sixth at the Drake Relays, and a little over a year later, ascended the world stage with his surprise third-place finish in the Olympic Trials.

At the Munich Olympics, Jenner placed second in the javelin and fourth in both the pole vault and 1,500 meters to place 10th overall. Not satisfied with his top-ten showing, Jenner spent the next four years preparing for a second shot at the Olympics—the Montreal Games in 1976. Jenner won the decathlon at the '76 Olympic Trials with 8507 points, breaking the world record he set the previous year. With personal best marks in eight of the ten events at the Montreal Games, Jenner amassed over 200 points more than silver medalist Guido Kratschmer to win the gold medal in a world record 8,618 points. Retiring from competition after the Montreal Games, Jenner gained further notoriety as an author, actor, spokesperson, and personality on the popular reality show *Keeping Up with the Kardashians*. Assigned male at birth, Caitlyn Jenner publicly came out as a transgender woman in April 2015, changing her name to Caitlyn. That same year Jenner received the Arthur Ashe Courage Award.

Jenner celebrates victory at the Montreal Games in 1976. (Rich Clarkson Collection)

Within moments of completing the 1,500 meters to secure gold in the decathlon, an exuberant spectator handed Jenner an American flag. The crowd roared and Jenner took a victory lap in celebration. The fan who handed Jenner the flag was Steve Elliot of Ellsworth, Maine. Twenty-three at the time and a former quarter miler at the University of Maine, Elliot leaped onto the track and evaded security to hand Jenner the Stars & Stripes.[12]

Eddie Hart

Eddie Hart equaled Jim Hines' world record of 9.9 in the 100-meter final at the Olympic Trials and earned a trip to the Munich Olympics. Among the favorites to earn the title of "World's Fastest Man" in Munich, Hart won his preliminary heats and advanced to the 100-meter quarterfinals. On the day of the quarterfinals, Hart and fellow US 100-meter qualifiers Rey Robinson and Robert Taylor were waiting for a bus to the stadium when their attention turned to a remote ABCTV monitor. The monitor showed the start of a 100-meter heat, and Hart asked the crew: "Say, they are showing the sprints. That a tape of the morning trials?"

"No, this is live, the first quarterfinal heat," Hart was told.[13]

The three US sprinters and coach Stan Wright rushed aboard an ABC studio van and sped to the stadium—only to arrive too late for Hart and Robinson. Taylor made his heat by mere seconds and with no warm-up, qualified for the semifinals. Wright later commented that he was working from an outdated event schedule and had not been informed the quarterfinals started nearly three hours earlier.

Eddie Hart, co-world record holder in the 100-meters in 1972, flies into the homestretch at Whittier Field. (Author's personal collection)

In his autobiography Disqualified, *Hart recalled fond memories of the training camp in Maine: "The people at Bowdoin were the friendliest I had ever met. There seemed to be a social event every day when we were there." Hart added, "Now, I do know something about lobster because it is my favorite food. We were in Maine two weeks, and I ate nine lobsters and hundreds of clams."*[14]

Hart would later win gold in Munich, running the anchor leg on the 400-meter relay and setting the world record with teammates Larry Black, Robert Taylor and Gerald Tinker. Tinker handed Hart the baton after building a five-meter lead, and even though Soviet Valeriy Borzov, the 100-meter gold medalist, was also on the anchor leg, Hart was not worried: "Borzov was not going to run me down, regardless, any more than I would have run him down if he had built the same lead, unless one of us pulled a muscle."[15]

Raised in the blue-collar town of Pittsburg, California, Hart learned from his parents the value of charity and perseverance—the same values that propelled him to a lifetime of success despite the heartbreak in Munich. He graduated from the University of California at Berkeley, and later earned a master's degree from California State University. Hart became a coach, teacher, author, and founder of the Eddie Hart All in One Foundation that supports underserved youth. Hart continued to compete as a masters runner and set a world record of 10.87 in the 100 meters at age 40; the record stood for 14 years.[17]

In another chapter of Hart's dramatic life story, his gold medal from the 400-meter relay was stolen in the 1970s but was returned about a year later. As reported by the *San Francisco Chronicle* in 2000, a man moving into an apartment found it in the corner of a closet and tracked down Hart.[17] "I guess you can't call it a miracle, but it's close" said Hart.[17]

Eddie Hart at the front during his qualifying round of the 100-meters in Munich. (Rich Clarkson Collection)

In the aftermath of his controversial disqualification at the Munich Games, many wondered how Hart would have stacked up against Borzov in the 100-meter final. In the opinion of Jimmy Hines, the gold medalist in the 100 meters in Mexico City, "Eddie had it all, including the mental approach. If he had gotten to the finals, it probably would have been a world record. He would have won without a doubt; he was faster than Borzov."[16]

From left to right, sprinters Larry Burton, Larry Black and Rey Robinson stride out at Whittier Field. (Courtesy of Portland Public Library Special Collections & Archives)

Rey Robinson

Rey Robinson qualified for the Munich Olympics as a 20-year-old competing for Florida A&M University. His rapid ascent to the world ranks was fostered by his father, Booker T. Robinson, a professional baseball player in the Negro Leagues and known for his speed around the bases.[18] Booker Robinson impressed upon his son that if he wanted to attend college, he had to get a scholarship. Following his father's advice, the star running back at Florida's Lakeland High School ran track his senior year and set national prep school records in the 100-yard and 200-yard dashes.[19] Robinson was named most valuable athlete at the Golden West high school championship meet in Sacramento where he met Bob Hayes, the 100-meter Olympic champion at the Tokyo Games and a Florida A&M alumn.[18]

Having tied the world record alongside Eddie Hart at the Olympic Trials, and with Robert Taylor only a step behind, Robinson believed the trio would sweep the 100 meters in Munich.[20] When learning of his disqualification and losing his only chance to compete for a medal, let alone a US sweep, Robinson unleashed his anger towards sprint coach Stan Wright who had taken responsibility for the mix-up: "The man's a coach…A man who lives by the stopwatch. Two 9.9 sprinters out of the Olympics! Do you dig that? Do you, man? Dig on that for a minute!"[21]

Like Eddie Hart, Robinson might have gained redemption as a member of the 400-meter relay team, but 200-meter runner Larry Black replaced him. Black was a strong curve runner and had competed as the lead-off man in a tune-up meet shortly before the Munich Games. Despite posting a world record time at the Olympic Trials, Robinson left Munich having only run one heat of the 100 meters.

After Munich, Robinson competed internationally and qualified for the Olympic Trials in 1976 and 1980 but finished out of the top three spots on both tries. He retired from running shortly after the 1980 trials and began a coaching career that led him back to Florida A&M as head coach of track and field. Robinson was also active as a leader and advocate for the National Youth Sports Program.[19]

Rey Robinson and sprint coach Stan Wright shortly before Robinson's disqualification in Munich. (Press Photo)

In a conversation with Eddie Hart in 2015, Robinson admitted, "I've gotten over what happened in Munich, too. I got that chip off my shoulder. I just outgrew it. I don't blame Coach Wright anymore."[20]

Robert Taylor

Robert Taylor was the last man standing after the controversial disqualification of 100-meter favorites Eddie Hart and Rey Robinson in Munich. Taylor made it to the starting line of his 100-meter quarterfinal heat, the third of the day, and had just enough time to pull off his sweats and quickly stretch before settling into the starting blocks. In the 100-meter final, he won the silver medal behind Soviet sprinter Valeriy Borzov, whose mechanics were so refined the press called him the "Russian Robot" and the "manufactured sprinter." Taylor won a second medal in Munich running the second leg on the gold-medal-winning 400-meter relay.

A native of Tyler, Texas, and collegiate standout at Texas Southern University, Taylor was the national AAU 100-meter champion in 1972 and was ranked No. 1 in the US by Track & Field News that same year. He was the third and final qualifier for the Munich Games at the Olympic Trials, finishing one-tenth of a second behind Hart and Robinson, who tied the world 100-meter record. After the Olympics, Taylor tried out for the Kansas City Chiefs, but as Porter Robinson, his former coach at TSU commented, "He had the speed, but he couldn't catch the ball."[22] Taylor then pursued a career in education teaching middle school, special education and physical education. He died of a heart attack in 2007 at age 59.

Sprinters Robert Taylor (left) and Gerald Tinker (right) jog in light rain at Whittier Field. (Courtesy of Portland Public Library Special Collections & Archives)

Robert Taylor (USA) leans to secure the silver medal behind 100-meter champion Valeriy Borzov of the Soviet Union. (Rich Clarkson Collection)

Eddie Hart, disqualified from the quarterfinals, watched the 100-meter final from the stands. Hart felt Taylor was burdened by his and Rey Robinson's absence from the finals: "He was carrying a lot of weight, which I think affected him negatively. When you watched him in that race, that wasn't Robert Taylor."[23]

Gerald Tinker

Gerald Tinker missed qualifying for the Munich Games in the 100 meters at the Olympic Trials, but his fourth-place finish earned him a spot on the 400-meter relay team. Held on the last day of the Games, the relay was also the last chance for the US sprint team to win gold after disqualification of Eddie Hart and Rey Robinson in the 100 meters, and two runner-up finishes to Valeriy Borzov in the 100 meters and 200 meters. After a strong start in the relay final by Black, and legs by Taylor and Tinker that extended the lead, the gold medal was all but assured as the baton landed in Hart's hand. The team won the event by a decisive three-tenths of a second to tie the world record the US already held.

Tinker's athletic prowess and determination led him across racial divides in both high school and college. At Coral Gables High School in Miami, Florida, Tinker was among the first black students to attend the formerly all-white school and was part of the first all-black backfield on the football team that won state championships in 1967 and 1968.[24] Memphis State University recruited Tinker who became the University's first black scholarship athlete in football and track.[25]

Gerald Tinker (left) and Robert Taylor (Right) sprint down the Bowdoin track. (Courtesy of Portland Public Library Special Collections & Archives)

At the training camp in Maine, Tinker roomed with his cousin and fellow Miami, Florida, native Larry Black, who would win silver in the 200 meters and join Tinker on the winning 400-meter relay team in Munich.

After the Olympics, Tinker transferred to Kent State University where he won the national indoor championship in the 60-meter dash in 1973 and was one of the university's top wide receivers and punt return specialists. Tinker graduated from Kent State in 1974, and later that year the Atlanta Falcons selected him in the second round of the NFL draft. The Falcons traded Tinker to the Green Bay Packers, and he retired from the NFL after the '75 season. Tinker became a professional trainer and coach for the fitness company he founded, Running Right.

Gerald Tinker (right) takes the baton from Robert Taylor to begin the third leg of the 400-meter relay. (Rich Clarkson Collection)

When Tinker handed the baton to anchor Eddie Hart, the race was a lock for the Americans. Tinker helped build such an insurmountable lead that Hart's leg became a formality. "That was my only race, and I wasn't going to fail at that. My friends told me that I built a five-meter lead; all I know is that it was the greatest race of my life," said Tinker.[26]

Sprinter Larry Black takes a breather on the infield at Whittier Field. (Author's personal collection)

Larry Black

Larry Black, an eleven-time All-American at North Carolina Central University, faced an uphill climb to Munich when he drew lane one in the 200-meter final at the Olympic Trials. As predicted, Black trailed Marshall Dill of Michigan State heading into the final stretch, but Black surged through the finish line to inch Dill out of third place and land a trip to the Olympics—both sprinters were timed in 20.6.[27]

Black and fellow 200-meter sprinters Chuck Smith and Larry Burton were among the favorites in Munich and had the talent to continue US dominance in the event. Americans had won gold in seven of the eight previous Olympic Games and had swept the 200 meters three times.[28] Soviet Valeriy Borzov, already Olympic champion in the 100 meters, had also been a favorite as the top sprinter in Europe for the previous three years. Prior to the Munich Games, the Soviets had never won an individual sprint medal, let alone gold.[28] The strong US 200-meter contingent had hoped to prevent Borzov from claiming both gold medals in the 100- and 200-meter sprint double.

In the finals of the 200 meters in Munich, Black once again drew lane one. But just as Black overcame the tight curve of lane one in the Olympic Trials, he came off the curve a half-step ahead of Borzov. Then, as described in the race recap by *Runner's World*, the disciplined Borzov did the unthinkable: "He glanced from side to side, then accelerated. He opened up a quick two-tenths of a second, and that was it."[29]

Larry Black, on the inside lane, sprints toward a silver medal in the 200 meters in Munich. (Rich Clarkson Collection)

As the lead-off runner on the winning 400-meter relay team, Black would add gold to his 200-meter silver medal. But Black remained unsettled about the 200-meter result and remarked: "He's fast man, but he didn't have to run in lane one. If I'd have run in lane five and Valeriy Borzov had run in lane one, Larry Black would have won."[29]

Larry Black, after winning the silver medal at the Munich Games in 1972. (Rich Clarkson Collection)

Black's life entered a tailspin shortly after the Olympics. Battling substance abuse and destitute, he pawned his gold and silver medals. A close friend of Black's, Tony Armstrong, returned the medals in late 1998. "I will never forget the pain I felt when I had to tell him [Armstrong] I didn't have my medals to show the kids anymore. Then I went to his house for his birthday over Christmas and he gave [me] my medals. I still get teary-eyed thinking about it. I had come full circle," said Black.[31]

Because of his strength running curves, Black replaced Rey Robinson on the lead-off leg on the 400-meter relay in Munich. Black hesitated to take away his teammate's last shot at a medal after Robinson's crushing disqualification in the 100 meters. "I know myself I've worried about Rey Robinson. I've replaced him on the relay and maybe I should let him run because he has no other chance to get a gold medal. It's been bothering me. Should I let him run? I still don't know what to do," said Black.[30] Black stayed on the team, which dominated the relay final, and defeated the Soviet team anchored by Valeriy Borzov.

After Munich, Black finished his degree at North Carolina Central and returned to his hometown of Miami, Florida, where he had planned to coach track.[31] Black married and moved from job to job until around 1979, when he became addicted to drugs and alcohol. "When the limelight of the Olympics disappeared, I was everywhere but nowhere with a bad element," said Black. "A weekend of drugs turned into a lifetime for me. Outside, I still looked like Larry the Olympian. Inside I was killing myself. …I was so proud of my Olympic medals, but I pawned them for drugs. People say, 'I could never do that,' but if you have ever been in the grips of something stronger than you have, never say never."[31]

Black turned his life around in 1994 after seeking refuge in a Miami homeless shelter that provided drug and alcohol treatment, and counseling. He remarried, found steady work at a Florida community fitness center and was a motivational speaker for youth groups. Black died of an aneurysm in 2006 at age 54.

200-meter sprinters Larry Burton and Larry Black match strides at Whittier Field. (Courtesy of Portland Public Library Special Collections & Archives)

Within eight months, Purdue sophomore Larry Burton ran his first track race, set a world record in the 60-yard dash, won the NCAA 200-meter national title and placed fourth in the Munich Olympics.

Larry Burton

Larry Burton had never run a track race until January of his sophomore year at Purdue University. A native of Melfa, Virginia, Burton was a star wide receiver at Mary N. Smith High School when Purdue recruited him in 1970. In the spring of his first year as a Boilermaker, Burton asked track coach Dave Rankin if he could join the track team, but Rankin told him it was too late in the season. During an interview with *Sports Illustrated* in 1992, Rankin recalled, "The next year he came up to me again. It was during the indoor season. December, maybe even January. I can remember him coming up to me on the track, saying, 'I would like to come out for the team.' This time I let him. I was a great recruiter, huh?"[32] That January, Burton tied the world record in the 60-yard dash (5.9) and capped his spring season with an NCAA national title in the 200-meters in 20.5.

At the Olympic Trials, Burton was the second qualifier for the US 200-meter squad that would compete at the Munich Games. With abundant raw talent and ranked fourth in the world in 1972, Burton was among the favorites in Munich and got off to a good start in the final. "I was out in front on the turn. I thought I was running the best race of my life. Never felt better. Then everyone came up and went past. Once that happened, there's no getting back. There's one shot," said Burton—he missed the bronze medal by half a stride.[32]

Burton returned to Purdue after the Olympics to finish his sociology degree. He continued to compete in football and track, earning multiple All-America honors and the Big Ten Medal of Honor for scholastic and athletic achievement. Burton graduated from Purdue in 1975 and entered the NFL draft. The New Orleans Saints selected him as the seventh overall pick, and he joined the receiving corps of star quarterback Archie Manning. Despite his speed, Burton fell short of expectations with only 35 catches and four touchdowns over three seasons with the Saints; injury prompted his release from New Orleans in 1978. Burton played two more seasons with the San Diego Chargers, including a playoff run in 1979, before retiring from football. "A voice told me, 'you're going to move on and do something different,'" remarked Burton.[32]

Burton and his wife Ida spent the next thirteen years as "family teachers" at the renowned Boys Town youth center in Omaha, Nebraska. Burton quickly became a valued teacher and counselor, affecting the lives of countless at-risk youth. In 1992, Burton left Omaha to lead a new Boys Town satellite in Long Beach, California, where he stayed until 2008.[33] Burton's grandson, Trey Burton, also played in the NFL and was part of the "Philly Special" scoring play that helped the Philadelphia Eagles defeat the New England Patriots in Superbowl LII (2017).

Larry Burton during his days as split end for the Purdue Boilermakers.[34] (Courtesy of Purdue athletics)

Before Purdue's matchup with Notre Dame in 1973, a reporter suggested that Burton might have trouble with the Notre Dame Secondary. Irish coach Ara Parseghian replied, "There are only three people in the world faster than Larry Burton, and they are not in the Notre Dame defensive backfield."[32]

Chuck Smith

Chicago native Chuck Smith prioritized academics while attending Occidental College in Los Angeles. But in 1970, his senior year, he raced in an intramural track meet, and Oxy track coach Dixon Farmer soon learned of Smith's raw talent.[28] In the weeks that followed, Smith won national collegiate titles in the 100 and 200 meters, and dropped his 200-meter time from 22.1 to 20.7. Following graduation, Smith competed for the Southern California Striders while attending graduate school at UCLA. Smith won the 200 meters at the AAU national championships in 1972 and continued his improbable journey by winning the 200 meters at the Olympic Trials.

Smith trained three hours a day honing his speed, stamina, and technique leading up to the Munich Games. "I've wanted that gold medal ever since 1968, when I watched Tommy Smith on television," said Smith.[6] Smith's dream of Olympic gold ended when he came down with the flu before the 200-meter final and placed fifth with a temperature of 105 °F.[35] Smith competed internationally through 1973 and retired soon thereafter.

Sprinters Chuck Smith (left) and John Smith (right) match strides at Whittier Field. (Courtesy of Portland Public Library Special Collections & Archives)

Smith enjoyed the comradery among his teammates at the training camp in Maine. In an interview with the Portland Press Herald *on July 23, 1972, he remarked, "There is a real bond between us because each of us knows what the other had to go through to get here. That's why athletes get along so much better than the countries that they represent."*[6]

John Smith

In 1971, John Smith set a world record in the 440-yard dash (44.5), won the 400 meters at the Pan American Games, and ended the year as the top-ranked quarter miler in the world. In 1972, Smith was the NCAA 400-meter champion and qualified for the Munich Olympics in the 400 along with Vince Matthews and UCLA teammate Wayne Collett. But the achievement that was to elude Smith was an Olympic medal.

The US 400-meter trio of Smith, Collett and Matthews were the top-ranked quarter milers in the world coming into the Munich Games. As reported by *The Boston Globe* shortly before the Munich Games, "The rest of the world has to look on at this sort of thing as hopeless resignation. Their own people keep getting faster and faster, but they still can't catch up to the Americans."[36] All three US sprinters qualified for the 400-meter final in Munich and were on their way to repeating the 1-2-3 medals sweep at the Mexico City Olympics. But on the first turn of the final, Smith pulled up with a torn hamstring and could not finish; Smith's teammates took home the gold and silver medals.

400-meter sprinter John Smith on the Bowdoin track infield. (Author's personal collection)

After Smith fell to the track with a torn hamstring in the Olympic 400-meter final, teammate Wayne Collett ran to where he was lying and held him in his arms. "He was inconsolable," recalled Collett.[40]

The Dallas Cowboys drafted Smith as a receiver after the Munich Games, but he returned to sprinting in 1974 as a professional in the track tour sponsored by the International Track Association (ITA).[37] The ITA folded in 1976, and as a professional athlete Smith could not compete for a spot at the Montreal Olympics. After a stint running professional track in Australia, Smith successfully petitioned to regain his amateur status and began training for the Moscow Olympics. Even before the US announced plans to boycott the Moscow Games, Smith ruptured his Achilles tendon and soon after retired from competition.[38]

Smith worked part time as an actor, model, and salesperson, then returned to the track in 1984—this time as a sprint coach at his alma mater, UCLA. During his 17-year tenure at UCLA and later with his own sprint team, Hudson Smith International (HSI), Smith's athletes have won 13 Olympic gold medals, 6 silver medals and 4 bronze medals.[39] One of Smith's sprinters, Steve Lewis, won gold in the 400 meters at the Seoul Olympics in 1988. Smith later commented, "It wasn't as if I'd won a medal of my own, but the fire, not dying, had let me help others."[40]

Vince Matthews

After running a 100-yard time trial, first-year student Vince Matthews failed to qualify for the track team at Andrew Jackson High School in Queens, New York.[41] He made the team a year later after trying a new event, the 440-yard dash. His first-ever quarter mile was 57.5, but after experiencing the pain of lactic acid late in the race, Matthews declared it would be the last time he would ever run a 440. Four years later, in 1968, he won an Olympic gold medal running the lead leg of the 1,600-meter relay at Mexico City.

Matthews was among the nation's top quarter milers in 1966 having run 48.0 in the 440 as a high school senior.[43] Matthews accepted a scholarship at Johnson C. Smith University in Charlotte, North Carolina, and by his sophomore year was ranked No. 2 in the world in the 400.[27] In 1968, at a pre-Olympic Trials meet in Echo Summit, California, Matthews set a 400- meter world record of 44.4. The record was later nullified because Matthews

From left to right: John Smith, Coach Stan Wright, Vince Matthews, Coach Hoover Wright and Chuck Smith at Whittier Field. (Courtesy of Portland Public Library Special Collections & Archives)

Bill Bowerman's team regimen at the Maine training camp included a 10:00 pm curfew that was tested early on by several of the sprinters. "Almost all the black athletes on the team were standing on the steps in front of a dormitory at Bowdoin College, jiving, joking and listening to some music on my tape recorder," recalled Matthews. "Just then, Bowerman walked out of the front door of the dorm and said in terse military tones, 'I told you guys I wanted everybody in by ten o'clock.'" The sprinters shrugged off the rebuke and lingered on the steps until Stan Wright coaxed the men back to their rooms.[42]

had worn an innovative, but illegal, "brush" shoe manufactured by Puma; each shoe contained 68 needle spikes, dozens more than the legal limit of six.[44] Two weeks later at the Olympic Trials in Echo Summit, Matthews went out too quickly and faded from first to fourth, finishing in 44.8. While short of his goal to compete in the open 400 at the Mexico City Olympics, Matthews' finish qualified him for the 1,600-meter relay team which set a world record 2:56:16.

After a year off from running, Matthews began training for the '72 Olympic Trials, where he qualified for the open 400 meters and the 1,600-meter relay at the Munich Games. Matthews breezed through the qualifying heats in Munich, then took command of the 400-meter final from the gun and held off teammate Wayne Collett to win gold in 44.66; Collett was runner-up in 44.80. During the medals ceremony, Matthews and Collett stunned the packed stadium as Collett, barefoot, joined Matthews on top of the podium where they talked, fidgeted, and looked around—all during the playing of the National Anthem.[43]

400-meter medalists Vince Matthews (left) and Wayne Collett (right) at the awards ceremony in Munich. (Rich Clarkson Collection)

Four years earlier in Mexico City, Matthews had watched from the stands as black sprinters Tommie Smith and John Carlos raised their fists and bowed their heads on the awards podium to protest racial injustice. Matthews wanted to make his own statement in Munich: "I know Wayne and I were doing something out of the ordinary—from not facing the flag to not standing at attention," said Matthews. "I knew that standing at attention for a song that didn't pertain to me wasn't for me."[45] The IOC banned Matthews and Collett from future Olympic competition, and with John Smith's injury the US could not compete in the 1,600-meter relay—an event the Americans were heavy favorites to win.

Matthews retired from competition after the Munich Games. Thirty-nine years later, he was elected to the National Track and Field Hall of Fame. He had been married to his wife Shirley for 37 years and owned an antique shop in Mount Vernon, New York.[43]

Vince Matthews glides to victory with teammate Wayne Collett close behind in the 400-meter final in Munich. (Rich Clarkson Collection)

Lee Evans

Until 1967, no runner had broken 45 seconds in the 400 meters. Then came Lee Evans, who ran 44.95 at the Pan American Games in Winnipeg, and a year later broke 44 to win the gold medal at the Mexico City Olympics. His time in Mexico City was 43.86—a world record that would stand for 20 years. Evans, along with teammates Vince Matthews, Ron Freeman, and Larry James, also won gold in the 1600-meter relay in Mexico City, and lowered the world record by a hefty three seconds. That record stood for 24 years when the US broke it again at the 1992 Olympics in Barcelona.

When Evans arrived in Brunswick, Maine, in July 1972, the gold medal champion and world record holder had only qualified to run a leg on the 1600-meter relay in Munich. Throughout 1972, Evans struggled with a hamstring injury, and at 25, was the oldest of the top 400-meter Olympic contenders at the Olympic Trials. In the 400-meter Trials final, Evans lagged from the start but closed strong enough on the homestretch to finish fourth and qualify for the 1,600-meter relay.[27] At the Munich Games, Evans lost his chance for a third career gold medal with the disqualification of all three of his teammates: John Smith because of his injury and failure to finish the open 400 meters, and Vince Matthews and Wayne Collett for their protest during the 400-meter awards ceremony. "What happened in Munich was like getting a divorce," Evans said. "I couldn't talk about it for five years. Two Olympic gold medals is nice, but three would have been better."[47]

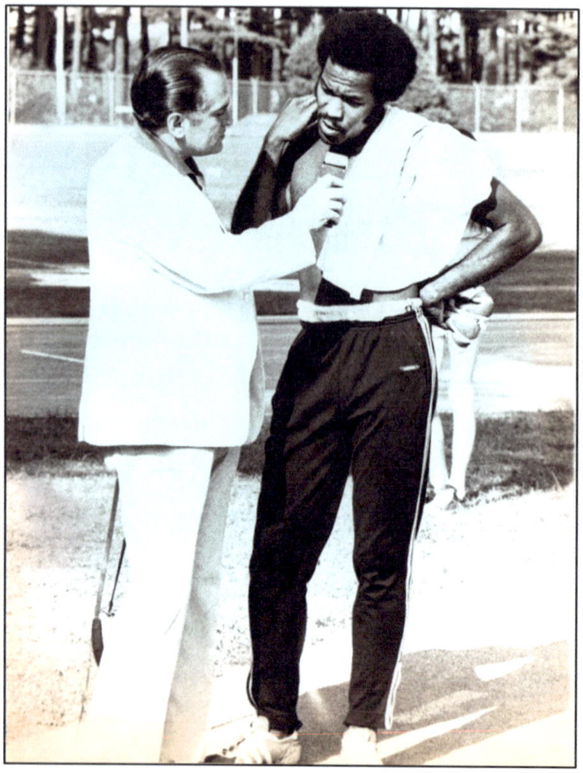

Lee Evans with a reporter at Whittier Field. (Author's personal collection)

Throughout his career, Evans leveraged his celebrity and media access to support the civil rights movement. While at San Jose State College in 1967, Evans spoke out against housing inequality for African Americans enrolled at the college.[46] Later that year, Evans became a founding member of the Olympic Project for Human Rights that promoted a boycott of the 1968 Mexico City games. After sweeping the 400 meters at Mexico City, Evans and his two teammates wore black berets on the awards podium in tribute to the Black Panther Party.[47] The trio removed their berets during the National Anthem and avoided possible disqualification from what was to be a world record setting 1,600-meter relay.

Lee Evans, 400-meter gold medalist at Mexico City, sprints the curve of the Whittier Field track. (Author's personal collection)

Dave Wottle, with his signature golf cap, during a workout at Whittier Field. (Courtesy of Portland Public Library Special Collections & Archives)

During his first workout upon arriving in Maine, Dave Wottle aggravated tendonitis in his left knee. "I did a hard workout that day. I guess it was too hard, because I haven't been able to work out seriously since then," said Wottle.[48] *Wottle thought his dream of a gold medal was over.*

Dave Wottle

Just 30 seconds into the 800-meter final in Munich, Dave Wottle was in last place. Wottle tied the world record of 1:44.3 in the Olympic Trials, but he had spent the previous month nursing severe tendonitis in his knee. "Unless I get in a few good workouts and races between now and the Olympics, I'll go into the races in Munich thinking I'm out of shape and can't stick with the pace," said Wottle.[48] But on the last lap of the Olympic final, Wottle passed the first of eight runners in the field, West German Franz-Josef Kemper. Wottle continued to slide up through the pack, and as the finishing straightaway approached, he had battled into fourth. Wottle unleashed his patented kick on the home stretch where he passed two Kenyans to take over second place. It seemed unlikely Wottle would catch gold-medal favorite Evgeni Arzhanov of the Soviet Union, but as the finish line drew near, Arzhanov stumbled and fell sprawling onto the track. The race appeared to be a dead heat until the official results had Wottle ahead by 0.03 seconds. It was the first gold medal for the US at the Munich Games.

Dave Wottle leans at the finish of the 800 meters and narrowly defeats the lunging Evgeni Arzhanov in Munich. (Rolls Press/Popperfoto via Getty Images)

Even with Wottle's world-record performance at the Olympic Trials, he was not the 800-meter favorite leading up to Munich. That distinction was held by Soviet Evgeni Arzhanov, who had not lost an 800 in three years.[49]

Wottle grew up in Canton, Ohio, where he began running in the eighth grade. After limited success as a sprinter, he focused on the mile and became the Ohio State Champion as a senior in 1969, running 4:20.[50] Wottle attended Bowling Green University and won the NCAA national 1,500-meter title in 1972. After winning the 800 meters at the Munich Olympics, Wottle returned to Bowling Green for his Senior year and won the NCAA outdoor championship in his favorite event, the mile, in 1973.[51] Wottle continued running as a professional and clocked a 3:53.3 mile in 1973—the third best time in the world, and second best in the US to Jim Ryun's world record 3:51.1.[51] Wottle retired from professional running in 1976 and became the track coach at Walsh College in Canton and later, Bethany College in West Virginia. He then became dean of admissions and financial aid at Rhodes College in Memphis, Tennessee, where he served for 29 years before retiring in 2012.[52]

Dave Wottle on the awards podium in Munich. (Rich Clarkson Collection)

As the national anthem played, Wottle forgot to remove his cap, and many thought it was an act of protest. "It just hit me like a ton of bricks. I remember getting teary-eyed and was very apologetic. I didn't know I had my hat on," explained Wottle.[53] The hat was a gift to Wottle in the spring of 1971, and it soon became a staple for keeping his unruly hair in place. The cap was inducted into the National Track and Field Hall of Fame in 1977, five years before Wottle himself.

Dave Wottle at Whitter Field. (Courtesy of Portland Public Library Special Collections & Archives)

Dave and Jan Wottle were married on July 15, 1972, just four days before the start of the training camp in Maine. Bowerman was dismayed at the timing of the wedding. "Dave Wottle is having a nice honeymoon, but he'll be lucky to get past the first round of the 800 meters," said Bowerman.[53]

After beating the odds and skepticism in Munich, Wottle commented: "Frankly, I was completely discouraged before the 800. I didn't think I had a chance. My wife talked me into that gold medal.[49]

Rick Wohlhuter

US 800-meter runner Rick Wohlhuter tripped and fell to the track in the first lap of his first race at the Munich Olympics. "I just remember that all of a sudden, I was down. First, I looked up at the crowd. Then I looked at the other runners and they weren't waiting for me," remarked Wohlhuter.[54] Wohlhuter sprang from the track and worked back to the lead pack but missed advancing to the semifinals by inches. Motivated by his misstep in Munich, Wohlhuter went on a racing campaign that led him to a half-mile world record of 1:44.6 in 1973, then 22 straight victories through 1974 that included a world record in the 1,000 meters.[55] Wohlhuter still holds the world record in the half-mile (1:44.1), and his 1,000-meter mark of 2:13.9 remains the American record after 48 years. In 1976, Wohlhuter competed at the Olympics in Montreal in the 1,500 meters and 800 meters. After running six races in nine days, he came away with a bronze medal in the 800 and placed sixth in the 1,500.

Sports Illustrated described Rick Wohlhuter as polite, mild-mannered, and on first impression "a nice guy who finishes last."[54] But on the track, Wohlhuter was dominant. He won two state championships in the half-mile as a high school runner in St. Charles, Illinois, then competing for the University of Notre Dame where he won the NCAA national title in the indoor 600 meters in 1970.[56] In 1980, Wohlhuter targeted a third Olympic appearance at the Moscow Games until the US boycott prevented American athletes from competing.[57] After retiring from racing in 1977, Wohlhuter worked as an insurance salesman in Chicago, and later, a financial consultant. In 1990, he became a member of the National Track and Field Hall of Fame.

Olympic 800-meter teammates Dave Wottle (left) and Rick Wohlhuter (right) at Whittier Field. (Courtesy of Portland Public Library Special Collections & Archives)

Rick Wohlhuter (USA) on his way to bronze in the 800 meters at the Montreal Games in 1976. (Rich Clarkson Collection)

Even after winning the Sullivan Award in 1974 as America's top amateur athlete, Wohlhuter told Sports Illustrated *he needed to come up with a name everyone would remember. "Wohlhuter is too tough. I need a name like, well, I saw a great one the other day," he said. When asked what it was, Wohlhuter replied: "I don't know. I thought it was great when I saw it, the kind people would never forget. But I forgot what it was."*[55]

Bob Wheeler

"No regrets, I tasted it," said Bob Wheeler, reflecting on his track career that led to the Olympics in Munich and a year of international racing in Europe.[58] Wheeler was a sophomore at Duke University when he qualified for Munich by placing third in the 1,500 meters at the Olympic Trials. Wheeler was less than a second behind Jim Ryun, the US middle-distance icon who held the world record in the mile at 3:51.1. Despite running a personal best in the 1,500-meter semifinals in Munich, Wheeler failed to advance to the final. With Ryun tripping in the first round of heats and Dave Wottle also missing the cut in the semifinals, the US was locked out of medal contention for the first time since 1956.[27]

Bob Wheeler proved a formidable competitor early on, running 1:49.9 for the 800 meters and 4:06.6 in the mile as a senior at Dulaney High School in Baltimore, Maryland. As a first-year student at Duke, he set the NCAA 1,000-yard indoor record in 2:07.4, and a little over a year later, he was competing in the semifinals of the 1,500 meters at the Munich Games. Wheeler took a leave of absence from college to compete in Europe and came away with a personal best in the 1,500 meters of 3:38.8.[58] Wheeler returned to Duke for his junior year, but after two surgeries for a bone spur and torn tendon, he retired from racing. After graduation, Wheeler turned his competitive energy into building a successful chain of retail athletic shoe outlets, later sold to Foot Locker.[59] Bob Wheeler was living in California when he passed away in 2010 at age 58.

1,500-meter runner Bob Wheeler works through the heat at Whitter field. (Courtesy of Portland Public Library Special Collections & Archives)

Olympic 1,500-meter qualifiers Bob Wheeler and Dave Wottle attended the training camp in Maine, leaving world record-holder Jim Ryun as the only qualifier not to attend.

Doug Brown

The air temperature was 94 °F, and the track was reportedly 135 °F when University of Tennessee 3,000-meter steeplechaser Doug Brown battled for a spot on the Olympic team during the '72 Trials.[27] Brown fell late in the race, but scrambled back to his feet in pursuit of third place runner Jim Dare of the US Navy track team. Brown passed Dare on the last lap then spurted into second on the finishing stretch, sandwiched between Oregon Track Club teammates Mike Manley (first) and Steve Savage (third). At the Munich Games, Brown finished ninth in his qualifying heat and out of contention for the final, which was won by Kenyan Kipchoge Keino in an Olympic Record 8:23.6.

Doug Brown clears a steeplechase barrier in his preliminary heat at the Munich Games. (Rich Clarkson Collection)

Known as "Mr. Everything" in distance running at the University of Tennessee, Detroit-native Doug Brown earned nine All-America honors in track and cross country from 1971 to 1974.[60]

After Munich, Brown returned to Tennessee where he won NCAA steeplechase titles in 1973 and 1974.[60] During his senior year, Brown set an American record in the steeplechase of 8:23.24—faster than the gold-medal winner at the Munich Games. Still hungry for another shot at the Olympics, Brown returned to Eugene for the Olympic Trials in 1976 where he qualified for the Montreal Games by winning the steeplechase 0.03 seconds ahead of Henry Marsh of Brigham Young University.[61]

At the Montreal Games, Brown lost his left shoe in the preliminary heats and missed qualifying for the final by two places. Brown qualified for the Moscow Olympics in 1980 but could not appear a third time at the Games because of the US boycott. In 1985, Brown succeeded legendary track coach Stan Huntsman at the University of Tennessee, and his teams won five Southeastern Conference track titles and the 1991 NCAA outdoor championship.[62] Brown served as an assistant US track and field coach for the 1996 Olympics in Atlanta, then coached at the University of Florida from 1996 to 2002.

Three-time Olympic steeplechase qualifier Doug Brown at Whittier Field. (Author's personal collection)

Steve Prefontaine

Ten days before arriving in Maine, 21-year-old Steve Prefontaine set the American record in the 5,000 meters at the Olympic Trials. Prefontaine's 13:22.8 ranked him fourth in the world behind Dave Bedford of Great Britain, Lasse Viren of Finland, and Ian McCafferty of Great Britain. But many thought Prefontaine's ability to push the pace from the front gave him an edge among the favorites competing in Munich.[63] Leading up to the 1972 Olympics, Prefontaine sharpened his speed with workouts that began with a solo 3:59 mile. "If everything goes right, and I feel good the day of the final, those guys are going to have to run like hell to beat me," said Prefontaine.[64]

On September 10, 1972, 13 runners got underway in the 5,000-meter final in Munich. Despite a field with world record potential, no one wanted to lead, and the pace through two miles was 8:56—slower than the 10,000-meter final.[65] With a mile to go, Prefontaine took control and dropped the pace from 67 seconds per lap to 62. The tortuous pace splintered the pack, leaving three battling for the front: Prefontaine, Viren and Mohammed Gammoudi of Tunisia. On the last lap, Gammoudi and Viren were in front and held off Prefontaine as he tried repeatedly to surge back into the lead. As the home stretch unfolded, an exhausted Prefontaine lost contact with his rivals leaving the gold medal for Viren and silver for Gammoudi. Prefontaine staggered over the last several meters and left room for Ian Stewart of Great Britain to claim the final medal. Prefontaine had run the last mile in 4:04 but finished a disappointing fourth. "It takes a lot out of me to accelerate and then fall back," said Prefontaine. "If I'd gotten by in the backstretch, I might have finished first or second..."[65]

Bowerman put Prefontaine's Olympic experience into perspective shortly after Munich: "He recognized that he was a kid running among men and the longer-distance races are men's races. I don't know of any distance performer who is not better at 25 than he was when aged between 18 and 22. He recognized his time was ahead of him."[66]

Steve Prefontaine strides in front of the grandstand at Whittier Field. (Courtesy of Portland Public Library Special Collections & Archives)

Looking ahead to the Munich Olympics, Prefontaine commented: "I want a race where it comes down to who's toughest, who can push himself the farthest into that kind of exhaustion where you have to whip yourself to go on."[65]

University of Oregon Legend Steve Prefontaine at Whittier Field. (Courtesy of Portland Public Library Special Collections & Archives)

Steve Prefontaine qualified for the Munich Games by winning the 5,000 meters at the 1972 Olympic Trials hosted at his home track. The race came down to a battle between the young Prefontaine and 34-year-old George Young, three-time Olympic veteran and bronze medalist in the steeplechase at the Mexico City Games. Young hung on until Prefontaine closed with a 58.7 final lap and opened a gap of nearly seven seconds to clinch the win.[27]

Prefontaine's world-class potential emerged soon after he began running cross country and track at Marshfield High School in Coos Bay, Oregon. During his junior year, he was undefeated in cross country and set a state record in the two-mile of 9:01.3. As a senior, he lowered his two-mile to a national record 8:41.5. Bowerman recruited Prefontaine to the University of Oregon, and by the end of his first year he had run an 8:40 two-mile, 3:57 mile and 13:22 three-mile to win his first of four NCAA Championships.[67] In June 1970, *Sports Illustrated* featured Prefontaine on the cover with the headline: "America's Distance Prodigy, Freshman Steve Prefontaine."

After his disappointment in Munich, Prefontaine followed through on his plan to skip the fall cross country season in 1972. Prefontaine had regained his hunger by the spring of his final track season in 1973, and he won a fourth NCAA three-mile championship in a collegiate record 12:53.4.[68] After graduating with a degree in Broadcast Communications, Prefontaine began working for the fledgling shoe company, Nike, as a public relations manager. Prefontaine joined decathlete Jeff Bannister, discus thrower Mac Wilkins and other athletes at clinics and sponsored events to promote the Nike brand.[69] The ITA offered Prefontaine nearly $100,000 per year in 1974 to join the professional track circuit, but he declined in order to keep his amateur status and a chance to compete in the Montreal Olympics.[69] That same year, Prefontaine set American outdoor records in the 3,000 meters, two-mile, 5,000 meters and 10,000 meters. The readers of *Track & Field News* voted Prefontaine the most popular track athlete in 1975, further solidifying his stature as an American running icon.

Steve Prefontaine takes charge in the Olympic 5,000-meter final, with the bearded Lasse Viren close behind. (Rich Clarkson Collection)

In the Munich final, Prefontaine surged to the front with a mile to go, but fell to the exhaustion he foretold, narrowly missing bronze and within two seconds of the gold medal.

On May 29, 1975, Prefontaine ran what would be his last race, an invitational 5,000 meters at the University of Oregon's Hayward Field. The race featured a contingent of Finnish runners and Frank Shorter, the marathon champion in Munich. Prefontaine won, narrowly missing his American record by 1.9 seconds. That evening, Prefontaine joined friends, family and coaches at a post-race gathering hosted by Geoff Hollister, one of Nike's first employees. In the early hours of May 30, shortly after dropping Frank Shorter off at Kenny Moore's house, Prefontaine died in a single-car crash—he was 24.

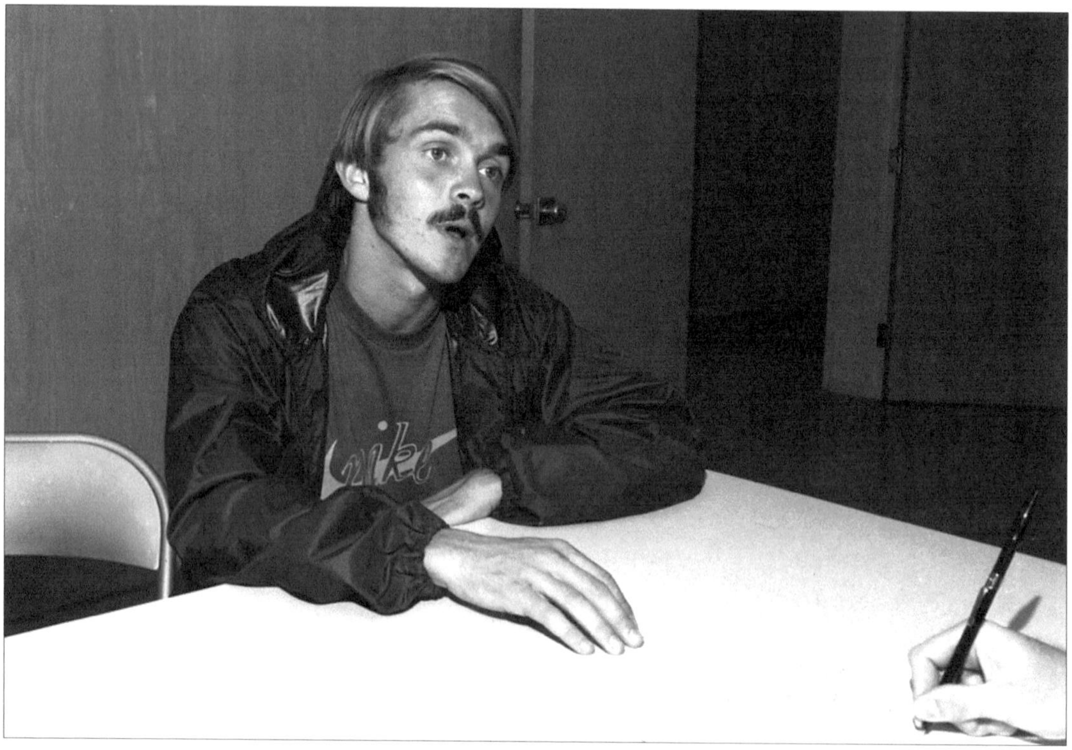

Steve Prefontaine during an interview with the *Portland Press Herald* on July 23, 1972. (Courtesy of Portland Public Library Special Collections & Archives)

In an interview with the Portland Press Herald, *Prefontaine spoke openly about the pressures of his sport. "If people started booing, or if I started to get in hassles like Jim Ryun, then I think I'd quit," said Prefontaine. "When your life isn't your own anymore, it's just not worth it."*[6]

Steve Prefontaine between intervals at Whittier Field. (Author's personal collection)

The US distance squad favored Adidas and Tiger racing shoes in 1972. But just weeks before the Olympic Trials, Bill Bowerman and Phil Knight began manufacturing shoes for a new company—Nike. Even though the swooshes quickly peeled off Prefontaine's first pair of Nike spikes, Jon Anderson won the Boston Marathon in a pair of Nike "Bostons" in 1973, and by the Montreal Olympics in 1976 annual sales were $7.5 million.[70]

Len Hilton

A native of Hillsboro, Texas, Len Hilton became the first Texan to break the four-minute mile, running 3:59.1 at his home track at the University of Houston in 1971.[71] A year earlier, Hilton ran the mile to anchor the University of Houston's world record-setting distance medley relay. But his appearance in the 1972 Munich Olympics was in the 5,000 meters, having placed third at the Trials in 13:40.2, 18 seconds behind winner Steve Prefontaine. Hilton failed to advance beyond the 5,000-meter qualifying heats in Munich and returned to competing in the mile after the Olympics. He won the AAU national outdoor mile championship in 1973, running a personal best 3:55.9 which ranked him No. 2 in the US behind Dave Wottle.[72] Hilton was the US national outdoor 1,500-meter champion in 1975, and retired from competition soon after.

Hilton graduated from the University of Houston in 1971 with a degree in engineering and became vice-president of operations at Kinder Morgan Energy. Hilton died from pancreatic cancer in 2000 at age 52.[71] Hilton is honored with the annual Len Hilton Memorial Track & Field Invitational hosted by the University of Houston.

5,000-meter qualifier, Len Hilton, trains on a cool day in Maine. (Courtesy of Portland Public Library Special Collections & Archives)

Even though Hilton competed in the 5,000 meters at the Munich Olympics, his specialty was the mile. During his career, Hilton broke the four-minute mile 32 times, and was ranked among the top four milers in the country in 1973, 1974 and 1975.[71]

Len Hilton of the Pacific Coast Track Club captures the national title in the 1,500 meters at Eugene, Oregon in 1975. (Press photo)

At the national meet in 1975, Hilton won the 1,500 meters in 3:38.3, which is equivalent to a 3:55 mile. Two years earlier, Hilton had run 3:55.9 to win the mile at the national championships hosted at Memorial Stadium in Bakersfield, California, with one key difference—the stadium had a dirt track.[73]

Olympic teammates (left to right) Jack Bacheler, Steve Prefontaine and Jeff Galloway on the track at Whittier Field. (Courtesy of Portland Public Library Special Collections & Archives)

Through years of competing among the best distance runners in the US, Galloway befriended many and grew especially close to Bacheler, Prefontaine and Shorter. His trip to Maine and the Olympics beyond was a rare opportunity to train, compete and represent the US as teammates. Reflecting on his experience in Maine, Galloway put it simply, "It was incredible."

Jeff Galloway

Jeff Galloway started running at 13 and describes himself as "…a fat kid who struggled to complete every workout."[74] But Galloway did not quit, and in 1963, near the end of his senior year at The Westminster Schools in Atlanta, Georgia, he won the two-mile state championship. Unrecruited, he ran track and cross country at Wesleyan University alongside future running legends Amby Burfoot and Bill Rogers and was an All-American in cross country his senior year. Galloway put plans to continue running after college on hold when he was selected No. 3 in the Vietnam War draft and enlisted in the Navy.[74] It was during his months at sea that Galloway visualized doing something great in his life—and greatness would come from running.[74]

Galloway entered graduate school at Florida State University after his release from the Navy in 1970. His goal was to prepare for a career in teaching and to embark on a two-year journey he hoped would lead to the Olympic Trials in 1972.[75] Galloway joined the renown Florida Track Club and began training with Frank Shorter and 1968 Olympian Jack Bacheler. His times improved dramatically, and in the spring of 1972, he qualified for the Trials in the marathon by running 2:20.03 at the Boston Marathon. Galloway then set his sights on qualifying for the 10,000 meters and the opportunity to race on the legendary Hayward Field track at the University of Oregon, the host site for the Trials. After eight weeks of grueling runs with Shorter and Bacheler at altitude in Vail, Colorado, Galloway lowered his 10,000-meter best by two minutes to run 28:29.9 at the US national meet in Seattle, Washington—he had qualified for his second event at the Olympic Trials.

The day of the 10,000-meter final in Eugene was blistering hot, and sticking to his plan to run cautiously, Galloway found himself in last place through the mile.[75] But as the race wore on, the field slowed and Galloway started picking off the faltering runners one-by-one. By the last mile, he had moved into second behind Shorter and held on easily to earn a spot on the Olympic team. In Munich, Galloway failed to advance from the qualifying heats and watched from the sidelines as Shorter and the rest of the field pushed Finland's Lasse Viren to a world record 27:38.4. Galloway would have had to lower his personal best by another 49 seconds to earn a medal.

Jeff Galloway and Florida Track Club teammate Jack Bacheler at Whittier Field. (Author's personal collection)

Galloway qualified for the 1972 Olympics in the 10,000 meters, but Bacheler struggled in the event and had only the marathon as his last chance to make the team. Determined that Bacheler would make the trip to Munich, Galloway ran by his side from start to finish and slowed at the line to assure his friend the third and final spot on the marathon team.

Jeff Galloway with sprinter Rey Robinson at Whittier Field. (Courtesy of Jeff Galloway)

Galloway and Robinson both lived in Tallahassee, Florida, leading up to the Munich Games, but the two had never met until the training camp in Maine.

Galloway continued to race at an elite level following the Munich Games, setting an American record in the 10-mile of 47:49 in 1973, followed by racing as a member of the US national track team that competed in Europe, Africa and the Soviet Union. He returned to Eugene in 1976 to run the Olympic Marathon Trials, placing ninth in 21:18:29. Four years later, he finished third in the Houston marathon in 2:16:36 at age 34.

In 1973, Galloway's passion for running led him to open Pheidippides, a running specialty store in Tallahassee, Florida. Fueled by the running boom, Galloway established over 35 Pheidippides franchise stores and launched a series of running clinics across the country. Galloway is widely known today as "America's Coach," and he has written 29 books on running that have reached over a million readers. A champion of the run-walk method, Galloway reached his 200th marathon at age 70.[76] Galloway lives in his native Atlanta, Georgia, where he continues to teach, write and run daily.

Among the leaders at the 1976 Peachtree Road Race are, left to right, Jeff Galloway, Bill Rodgers and Don Kardong. (Courtesy of Atlanta Track Club)

In 1970, Galloway won the first Peachtree Road Race held in Atlanta, Georgia. Recognized as the world's largest road race, Peachtree has grown from a field of 110 in 1970 to 60,000 today. As a race organizer in the late-1970s, Galloway played a key role in Peachtree's success by recruiting world-class athletes including Shorter, Viren, Rodgers and Kardong.

Olympic 10,000 meter and marathon qualifier Frank Shorter at Whittier Field. (Author's personal collection)

Shorter roomed in Bowdoin College's Maine Hall during the training camp in 1972, fitting accommodations given his connections to the state before and after the Munich Games. As a youth, Shorter often visited Tenants Harbor, the village where his mother and artist, Katherine Chappell Shorter, owned a summer cottage.[77] Shorter returned to Maine in 1998 as an honorary meet director at the Maine Distance Festival hosted at Whittier Field. In 2012, he joined fellow Olympic marathon gold-medalist Joan Benoit Samuelson and marathon great Bill Rodgers to run the race founded by Samuelson—the Beach to Beacon 10K. Four years later, Shorter received an honorary degree at Bowdoin's 211th Commencement.

Frank Shorter

At mile nine on the twisting marathon course in Munich, Frank Shorter accelerated and left the field behind. "I told myself to get as far ahead as I could because if I got far enough ahead, I honestly thought no one would catch me," remarked Shorter.[78] And no one did. Shorter won the marathon in 2:12:19.8 and finished over two minutes ahead of the field that included defending Olympic champion Mamo Wolde of Ethiopia and world record holder Ron Hill of Great Britain. After crossing the finish line, Shorter did not have to wait long to embrace his teammates, Kenny Moore and Jack Bacheler, who placed fourth and ninth, respectively, in the best finish ever for the US in the Olympic marathon. Shorter's gold medal was the first for an American since Johnny Hayes' marathon victory at the London Games in 1908.

Shorter's decisive race tactics and insurmountable lead that followed made his marathon win look easy. Shorter later recounted that the only real threat to his victory was in the first mile when a busload of photographers nearly ran him over.[79] But the Olympic marathon in Munich was only Shorter's fifth race at 26.2 miles, and he was a dark horse among the more seasoned veterans. Even with a growing lead as the race in Munich wore on, Shorter was reluctant to believe he could win. "I never wanted to think of myself as a possible winner. I was concentrating on resisting to the very end," said Shorter. "If one does it, he risks spoiling things."[80]

Shorter's path to gold began when, at 127 pounds, he quit as a halfback on the Mount Herman High School football team and tried running. During his junior year in 1964-1965, Shorter was undefeated in cross country and won the two-mile at the New England outdoor track championships.[82] As a collegiate

Frank Shorter cruises to gold in the Olympic Marathon in Munich. (Rich Clarkson Collection)

When Shorter entered the stadium with a gold medal all but guaranteed, he heard tremendous applause, followed by whistling and boos. Shorter later learned that a West German student, Norbert Sudhaus, had run onto the track ahead of him in a perfectly timed prank. Shorter commented later, "He stole my entrance, all right, but that didn't really matter much. These Olympics were so battered by the bizarre and the tragic that I couldn't get worked up over an imposter."[81]

Frank Shorter among the leaders in the 10,000-meter final in Munich. (Rich Clarkson Collection)

Overshadowed by his stunning win in the marathon, Shorter also competed in the 10,000 meters where he placed 5th in 27:51.4—an American Record.

runner at Yale University, Shorter lacked focus and after three years of mediocrity, head coach Bob Giegengack told him: "If you train hard and make a commitment, you could probably make the Olympic team. But you'll have to give it all your time. And cut out the skiing, the singing, and the sunning."[83] Giegengack, who had been coach of the US track and field team at the Tokyo Games, was respected by Shorter who embraced the challenge. During his senior year, Shorter was an All-American in cross country, and on the track, he ran 4:06 in the mile and 8:45 in the two-mile before winning the NCAA outdoor six-mile championship in 29:00.

After graduating from Yale in 1969, Shorter began running twice a day and increased his workload to over 100 miles per week, often training at altitude.[84] Shorter won his first of four AAU national cross country championships in 1970, and the following year he completed his first marathon at the AAU Championships in Eugene, Oregon, where he placed second in 2:17:45. Six months later, he won Japan's Fukuoka Marathon in 2:12:50—the fastest marathon in the world in 1971. At the '72 Olympic Trials, Shorter won the 10,000 meters and tied for first in the marathon. Even though betting odds still favored Ron Hill of Great Britain to win the Olympic marathon, Shorter's rapid ascent could not be ignored. "Shorter, an old Yalie, has simply never been tested, really," wrote *The Boston Globe* columnist Jerry Nason. "Frank Shorter could make history."[85]

After his victory in Munich, Shorter sought to distance himself from the prospects of endorsements and limelight as a celebrity. His focus was to complete his law degree and train to defend his marathon gold at the Montreal Games in 1976. Widely favored to win in Montreal, Shorter became perplexed late in the race when a runner he did not recognize, East Germany's Waldemar Cierpinski, pulled away with ease to win the race; Shorter placed second in 2:10:46, nearly two minutes faster than his effort in Munich. Cierpinski was later implicated in his country's state-sponsored doping program, but he still holds the gold medal.[86] Shorter became a prominent voice for integrity in sports and was chair of the US Anti-Doping Agency from 2000 to 2003.

Shorter competed at an elite level through 1980 when injury forced a pullback from major competition. Widely credited with igniting the running boom with his marathon win in Munich, Shorter has remained influential as a sports commentator, motivational speaker, author, and advocate for mental health and victims of child abuse.

The Munich marathon team in Maine (left to right): Kenny Moore, Frank Shorter, Jack Bacheler and alternate Jeff Galloway. (Author's personal collection)

Fans at Whittier Field were treated with an intimate view of the '72 Olympians in action. Training camp officials also encouraged local runners to join the US men's distance team for "social" runs on the road. One local, Jerry Crommett, pushed the pace at the end of a long run and annoyed Shorter and Bacheler who nicknamed him the "green weenie" for the bright green socks he wore. The duo retaliated with an acceleration over the last 400 meters that left Crommett far behind.

Kenny Moore

Kenny Moore was the only US distance athlete to arrive in Maine with Olympic marathon experience. That came at the Mexico City Games in 1968, where Moore placed 14th in 2:29:49. Moore had been in medal contention until mile 17 when he developed severe blisters from athletic tape wrapped around the balls of his feet.[87] Moore had taken the advice of a trainer to try a new breathable tape, and violated an important rule taught by his college coach, Bill Bowerman: *do nothing new in a big race.*

Just two years after his painful Olympic debut, Moore ran 2:11:36 to set an American record at the Fukuoka marathon in Japan. By the end of 1970, Moore became the top-ranked marathoner in the US. The following year, he encouraged his training partner, Frank Shorter, to try the marathon at the AAU nationals. "I won by a minute in 2:16:48," commented Moore, "Frank would not lose another marathon for five years."[88] Moore qualified for the Olympic marathon in Munich by tying with Shorter at the Olympic Trials in 2:15:57. Shorter would win the marathon in Munich, while Moore hung on to fourth despite suffering from dehydration and injuries to both his hamstrings in the last miles.

Moore claimed to have never won a race as a runner at North Eugene High School in Oregon.[89] But at the University of Oregon, he blossomed under the tutelage of coach Bill Bowerman, and became an All-American in cross country and track. Moore embraced high mileage throughout college, including daily runs up to 30 miles beginning his sophomore year. After graduating in 1966, Moore leveraged his base of strength and endurance to win an AAU national cross country championship in 1967, six straight victories in San Francisco's Bay to Breakers 12K road race (1968 to 1973), and a string of marathons that would lead him to the Olympic Games in Mexico City and Munich. At age 33, Moore aimed for a third Olympic appearance at the Montreal Games, but the onset of pneumonia forced him to withdraw just week before the Trials.[90]

Kenny Moore embraces Frank Shorter after narrowly missing the bronze medal in Munich. (Rich Clarkson Collection)

Reflecting on the medal he missed, Moore wrote, "I walked the Munich infield trying to know how to react. The thought came of what [coach] Bob Newland would always tell us back in high school: 'Lift up your head. You ran the hardest you humanly could.'"[91]

Kenny Moore and Mamo Wolde on the marathon course in Munich. (Jerry Cooke/*Sports Illustrated* via Getty Images)

Near the end of the marathon, Moore and Wolde shared a brief but poignant encounter that stirred Moore to action 23 years later. Moore recalled: "...with five miles to go, a dehydration cramp shot up my right hamstring. Mamo watched me slow and hop, grabbing my leg, and then he turned and ran on. He looked back one last time. This is what I cannot forget. His face was filled with regret. He seemed to be saying it wasn't supposed to happen this way. We were supposed to race on together, and the stronger would take the silver and the other the bronze."[92]

Throughout his Olympic quest, Moore never lost focus on his writing and his ambition to become an impactful sports journalist. On his way to a master's degree in creative writing in 1971, Moore began writing for Eugene's Register-Guard and soon caught the attention of *Sports Illustrated.*[89] Moore began working for the magazine in 1972, and became the lead track and distance running correspondent. Moore left *Sports Illustrated* in 1995, shortly after crafting one of his most powerful narratives—the story of Mamo Wolde, the Ethiopian marathoner who won gold at the Mexico City Games and bronze in Munich.[92] As an army officer under the former communist regime in Ethiopia, Wolde was accused of being involved in the execution of a young rebel and was imprisoned in 1991. Moore undertook a harrowing journey to visit Wolde in prison and joined scores of advocates around the world who pleaded for his release. Wolde's freedom would not come until nearly six years later when the Ethiopian government found him guilty of a lesser charge, and released him for time already served at an age near 70.[93]

While continuing to write for *Sports Illustrated*, Moore began acting and played a supporting role alongside Mariel Hemingway in the movie *Personal Best* (1982). *Personal Best* opened to mixed reviews, but Moore received praise from critic Vincent Canby: "The film's biggest surprise is Kenny Moore, who plays the former athlete who falls in love with Chris Cahill [played by Hemingway] and who saves her from a well of loneliness."[94] Moore later co-wrote the film *Without Limits* (1998) with Oscar-winning director Robert Towne. Produced by Tom Cruise, the popular W*ithout Limits* is a biopic on the late running icon Steve Prefontaine and his relationship with his coach, Bill Bowerman.

Shortly after Bowerman's death in 1999, Moore rented a cottage in Eugene, Oregon, and began writing the deeply insightful and often personal story of Bowerman's life.[95] Published in 2006, *Bowerman and the Men of Oregon: The Story of Oregon's Legendary Coach and Nike's Cofounder,* received critical acclaim as one of the best books on running. Moore received the George Hirsch Journalism Award in 2012, and at the ceremony, Maine native and Olympic marathon champion Joan Benoit Samuelson remarked, "I can't think of another writer who has covered the sport with such passion, knowledge, and honor."[96] Moore died peacefully at his home in Kailua, Hawaii, on May 4, 2022, at age 78.

Jack Bacheler

When Frank Shorter sought a training partner to prepare for the Munich Olympics, he picked arguably the hardest working runner in the US—Jack Bacheler. After graduating from Miami University in Ohio where he was a two-time All-American in cross country and track, Bacheler moved to Gainesville, Florida, to pursue a Ph.D. in entomology. There he joined the nascent Florida Track Club and began logging 100-plus miles per week in Florida's oppressive heat and humidity. In 1968, Bacheler qualified for the Mexico City Games in the 5,000 meters and was the only US runner to earn a spot in the finals; a bout of dysentery squashed his chance to compete for a medal. In 1969, Bacheler won the national AAU 6-mile championship and became the top-ranked US runner in the two-mile, three-mile and six-mile. That same year Bacheler ran his personal best in the mile—4:01.3.[97] Bacheler soundly defeated Shorter in the '69 AAU six-mile championship, and Shorter decided soon after to move to Gainesville and train with the tall, resolute entomologist. "Jack, more than anyone, helped me to become a better runner," remarked Shorter.[98]

US Distance Team Members at Whittier Field (Left to right): Jack Bacheler, Steve Prefontaine and Jeff Galloway. (Courtesy of Portland Public Library Special Collections & Archives)

At just over 6-6, Bacheler played basketball until his senior year in high school when his mediocre shooting and rebounding led him to try running.[97] In the spring of 1962, Bacheler finished third in the mile at the state meet in 4:28, and the University of Miami in Ohio offered him a scholarship. Six years later he was in the Olympic final of the 5,000 meters.

With the '72 Olympic Trials a little over two months away, Bacheler joined Shorter and Galloway in Vail, Colorado, where the trio trained at altitude and ran two to three times a day, often covering 20 miles or more.[99] The effort paid off for Shorter and Galloway, who both qualified for the Munich Games in the 10,000 meters, and for Shorter, the marathon as well. But Bacheler struggled in the 10,000, losing the third and final qualifying spot to Jon Anderson, who surged past him on the last straightaway to the delight of Anderson's hometown fans in Eugene. Meet officials also disqualified Bacheler for bumping into Anderson and stripped him of his fourth-place finish and a slot as an alternate. Shorter and Galloway were despondent and saw only one way Bacheler could join them in Munich—the marathon.

Bacheler had qualified for the Olympic Trials marathon by winning his first marathon, Atlanta's Peach Bowl, in 2:22:00. On the last day of the Olympic Trials, Bacheler was among the 100 runners who started on Eugene's marathon course for a last try at the Munich Games. Under hot and humid conditions, the field thinned out quickly, leaving Shorter and Kenny Moore in control of the top two spots, and Galloway and Bacheler paired up for third and fourth. After tying with Moore for the win, Shorter watched anxiously as his two training partners entered the Hayward Field stadium. "They arrived next, sharing third—but who would get it?" recalled Shorter. "As they neared the finish, Jeff eased off, assuring Jack's position on the team."[100]

Jack Bacheler (center) with Florida Track Club teammates Frank Shorter (shirtless) and Jeff Galloway (front left). (Courtesy of the Florida Track Club)

Bacheler was a founding member of the Florida Track Club and designed the club's iconic Florida orange logo.

In the Olympic marathon in Munich, Bacheler worked his way into fifth place, but suffered painful swelling of his feet in the late miles and finished ninth. "My feet swelled up but my shoes didn't," said Bacheler. "I lost all my toenails but one."[101] After Munich, Bacheler became a professor of entomology at North Carolina State University where he remained until his retirement in 2013. Bacheler also coached at North Carolina State where he led the women's cross country team to national championships in 1979 and 1980. Despite his success as an entomologist and coach, Bacheler longed to continue his journey as a competitive runner. In 2001, Joan Nesbit of *Runner's World* asked him about his transition from running to the next phase of life. "I never did," replied Bacheler. "It's as if someone accidentally died and I never got the chance to say what I wanted to say…to say goodbye."[101]

Goetz Klopfer

Race walking is not rocket science unless your name is Goetz Klopfer. Formerly employed by NASA as an aerospace engineer, Klopfer refers to "center of gravity" and "altitude" when describing race walking technique.[102] While working for Seattle-based Boeing on the Super Sonic Transport project in the late-1960s, Klopfer climbed the US and world rankings in distance race walking.[103] In 1968, he placed second in the Olympic Trial 50-kilometer race walk at Echo Summit, California, in 4:44:32 and qualified for the Games at Mexico City. In the 50 kilometers at Mexico City, Klopfer was in 17th place at the half-way mark, then surged in the second half to finish 10th overall in 4:39:13.8. Klopfer made a second Olympic appearance at the Munich Games in the 20-kilometer event where he finished 19th in 1:38:33.6.

Born in Merseburg, East Germany, Klopfer immigrated with his family to the US in the early 1950s and attended Bloomfield Hills High School, just outside Detroit.[103] He joined the track team as a high hurdler, but soon moved to the half-mile and started running cross country. Klopfer first tried race walking during his sophomore year in 1963. Four years later, he qualified for his first international competition, the Pan American Games, where he won bronze in the 50 kilometers. In 1971, Klopfer returned to the Pan American Games and won the gold medal in the 20 kilometers. Over the course of his career, Klopfer set American records in eight race walking events ranging from 25 kilometers to 25 miles, and he recorded what was then the longest distance covered in a two-hour walk—15 miles and 1,578 yards.[104]

Olympic race walker Goetz Klopfer at Whittier Field. (Author's personal collection)

In June 1963, Sports Illustrated's *"Faces in the Crowd" featured Klopfer: "Goetz Klopfer, a sophomore at Michigan's Wayne State, heeled and toed his way to victory over nine others to win the state's AAU 12-kilometer walking race, despite being stopped by a Detroit patrol car and issued a $5 ticket for 'walking on the road.'"*[105]

After the Munich Games, Klopfer completed his doctorate at Berkeley and accepted a postdoctoral assignment with NASA in Mountain View, California. In 1976, he attempted to qualify for his third Olympics at Montreal but placed sixth in the 20-kilometer trial and retired from elite competition shortly after. Nearly 40 years later, fellow Olympic race walker Tom Dooley convinced the 73-year-old Klopfer to compete in the World Masters Athletic Championships in Lyon, France; Klopfer took home a bronze medal for his age group in the 20-kilometer walk.

Tom Dooley

Race walking champions Tom Dooley and Goetz Klopfer had both competed at Mexico City in 1968, but the Munich Games would be their first head-to-head Olympic competition. Dooley competed in the 20-kilometer walk in Mexico City, finishing 17th, while Klopfer competed in the 50 kilometers and placed 10th. The two lifelong friends and training partners first met in California during college—Dooley at San Jose State and Klopfer at Stanford.[106] As reported by *Heal and Toe Online*, "Starting in 1966, they have trained together…race walking the 40-mile round-trip on public streets between their respective schools on weekends."[107] In Munich, it was Dooley who prevailed, finishing 15th, just four places ahead of Klopfer. Dooley's 1:33:58.8 was six minutes faster than his race walk at altitude in Mexico City and would have virtually tied for the gold medal won by Soviet Volodymyr Holubnychy at the '68 Games. Like Goetz, Dooley attempted to qualify for the Montreal Games in 1976, but fell short with an eighth-place finish in the 20-kilometer race walk trial.

Tom Dooley and training partner Goetz Klopfer work out at Bowdoin. (Courtesy of Portland Public Library Special Collections & Archives)

A native of San Francisco, Dooley was a miler and cross country runner in high school and college, but became hooked on race walking when he won a mile walking event at an all-comers meet in 1965.[106] Dooley set 11 national race-walking records and won four national titles between 1967 and 1975. He won a silver medal in the 20 kilometers at the Pan American Games in 1971, 46 seconds behind the winner, Klopfer.

Dooley became a high school history teacher in the San Francisco Bay Area where he taught for 36 years. In 1994, he began serving as the national coach for Team in Training, the fundraising program for the Leukemia & Lymphoma Society. The charity has raised over a billion dollars through pledges earned by marathon walkers.[108] During an interview in 2018, Dooley commented, "They called me up because, they said, 'We heard you knew how to walk.'" Dooley retired after 25 years with Team in Training and continues to compete in masters race walking events. He plans to race in the World Masters Track and Field Championships in Tampere, Finland in 2022—alongside his steadfast friend, Goetz Klopfer.

Steve Hayden

On July 4, 1972, Steve Hayden stepped up to the starting line of the 50-kilometer race walk at the Olympic Trials having competed in the race only once. After failing to qualify for the 20 kilometers three days earlier, Hayden was uncertain whether he would compete in the grueling 50 kilometers. At last, he entered to help pace his Long Island Athletic Club teammate, Gary Westerfield. But as the race wore on, Hayden left Westerfield behind and finished a surprising third in 4:23:22, 34 minutes faster than his first try at the 50. "With his easy style and completely relaxed attitude he [was] just moving along and suddenly found himself with nothing to do but go ahead and win a trip to Munich," wrote the *Ohio Racewalker*.[109] At the Munich Games, Hayden could not match his insouciant performance at the Trials and settled for 27th place in 4:36:07.

Olympic 50-kilometer race walker, Steve Hayden at Whittier Field. (Courtesy of Portland Public Library Special Collections & Archives)

While training in Maine, Hayden roomed with race walking legend Larry Young, the last American race walker to win an Olympic medal—bronze in 1968 and 1972. In Maine, the two 50-kilometer qualifiers, one from New York and the other from Missouri, trained together for the first time. "We went out on three-hour strolls, but it was more relaxing for Larry than it was for me," remarked Hayden.

Hayden was a state champion cross country runner at Long Island's Wantagh High in 1961 and continued running while attending Penn State University from 1961 to 1966. He first tried race walking at a recreational event in 1967 and had no plans to continue until he met American race walking great, Henry Laskau, wo made an encouraging remark on his natural ability.[110] Hayden went on to place in national competition from the mile to the 50 kilometers and qualified for the US team that competed in the Lugano World Cup hosted by West Germany in 1970. Leading up to the '72 Olympic Trials, Hayden focused solely on his training and work as a middle school math teacher. "There are many things a guy my age could be doing," said Hayden. "But that is where personal sacrifice comes in, I have no regrets."[110]

In 1974, Hayden became a leading advocate in the movement to protect race walking from expulsion at the Montreal Games. Hayden helped form the *Committee for the Retention of Olympic Walking* and his old friend, Henry Laskau, joined the cause.[111] While the 20 kilometers persevered, the organizers of the Montreal Games dropped the 50, an event contested at the Olympics since 1932. The 50 kilometers returned to Moscow in 1980, but in 2021, the IOC voted to replace race walking's marathon with a mixed team event beginning at the Paris Games in 2024. Olympic organizers cited gender equity as the driver for replacing the 50 since the Games did not offer a women's version.[112]

Olympic 50-kilometer team member Bill Weigle and an unidentified runner on the track at Whittier Field. (Courtesy of Portland Public Library Special Collections & Archives)

Bill Weigle

Bill Weigle did not believe in half measures. He completed a degree in chemistry from Dickinson College where he was ranked No. 1 in his class, then went on to earn a Ph.D. in atmospheric sciences from the University of Michigan in 1973. Weigle began running in 1968, and by 1971 he was logging up to 100 miles a week at altitude in Boulder, Colorado.[113] In early 1971, he moved from running to endurance race walking. After only four months in the sport, he was runner-up in the Junior National 10-kilometer walk in 51:08. Precisely a year later, on July 4, 1972, Weigle competed in the 50 kilometers at the Olympic Trails alongside race walking greats Larry Young, Bob Kitchen and Steve Hayden. Weigle passed US record-holder Bob Kitchen in the last 10 kilometers and held on to second place behind winner Larry Young.[27] Young set a new American Record of 4:13:04.4; Weigle was timed in a personal best 4:20:09.4. At the Munich Games, Weigle finished 17th in 4:22:52.2.

Weigle continued to compete after the Olympics, winning the national championship in the 50 kilometers in 1973 and earning a No. 2 ranking in the US 50-kilometer race walk for the second year in a row.[113] In 1980, at age 40, Weigle competed in the Western States 100-mile endurance event, placing 3rd in 19:53:30—an average pace of 11:56 per mile.

Weigle has bicycled solo across the Northern Tier States and hiked the rim of the Grand Canyon twice. A retired professor of mathematics and environmental studies, Weigle has been active in preserving the wilderness near his home in Marina, CA. "I like the solitude I get out there. I like that there are nice rolling hills to walk – I love to walk hills – and I think the scenery is incredible," said Weigle. "Being outdoors—running, bicycling or walking—has really been my passion."[113]

110-meter hurdler Rod Milburn at Whittier Field.
(Author's personal collection)

Rod Milburn

In 1971, high hurdler Rod Milburn was unbeaten in 28 races and swept the NCAA, AAU and National Association of Intercollegiate Athletics (NAIA) championships. At the AAU meet, he became the first in the world to run 13.0 in the 120-yard hurdles, breaking a 13-year-old record by two-tenths of a second. When asked by *Sports Illustrated* about his chances at the Munich Olympics, Milburn replied, "A trackman is like a flower, you have to bloom again every spring. I've got to go to work and do it all over again."[114] Milburn's work led to virtual perfection in every heat of the 110-meter hurdles he ran in Munich. In the final, he won in 13.24, tying a world record which would stand for another five years. Milburn's teammates, Tom Hill and Mexico City gold medalist Willie Davenport, were both clocked in 13.5, but the finish line photo favored Hill for the bronze medal.

Milburn was born in the racially divided town of Opelousas, Louisiana, and honed his championship form on a grass track at J. S. Clark High School.[115] In 1969, Milburn tied the high school national high hurdle record as a senior and earned a scholarship at Southern University in Baton Rouge. Milburn was a sophomore at Southern University when he went undefeated in the hurdles and was honored by *Track & Field News* as Athlete of the Year.[116]

Milburn was the favorite to win the 110-meter hurdles at the '72 Olympic Trials, but he struggled in the final and was among four competitors timed in 13.6. Third place went to Milburn in the photo finish, securing him a place on the starting line in Munich. Milburn later explained someone stole his wallet at the AAU national meet in Seattle, just before the Olympic Trials. After borrowing money for the trip back to Southern University, he learned a dormitory fire had destroyed all his possessions. As reported by *The Boston Globe*, "He was a psychological wreck for the race."[117]

Following Munich, Milburn dominated the hurdles as a professional competing on the ITA. The ITA folded in 1976, leaving Milburn ineligible to compete at the Montreal Games as a former paid athlete. The AAU reinstated Milburn's amateur status in 1979, but the US boycott of the Moscow Games in 1980 eliminated his chance for a second appearance at the Olympics.

Rod Milburn floats over the high hurdles at Whittier Field. (Courtesy of Portland Public Library Special Collections & Archives)

Many attributed Milburn's dominance in the early 1970s to his unorthodox style of hurdling with both hands thrust forward during take-off. "...he had a lot of explosion," remarked rival Renaldo Nehemiah. "He was the first hurdler ever to sprint between the hurdles, not just three steps and a jump."[118]

Milburn retired from competition in 1983 and became coach of track and field at Southern University a year later. After Southern cut Milburn's coaching position in 1987, he began working at Georgia Pacific's Port Hudson pulp and paper mill. Even after nearly a decade of steady work at the mill, Milburn struggled financially and had to grapple with a divorce filed by his wife. In 1996, his estranged wife moved his medals, trophies and mementos into a commercial storage facility and after the rent lapsed, Milburn's possessions—including his Olympic gold medal—were auctioned to the owner of a thrift store.[115] Milburn had arranged to recover his belongings on November 13, 1997, but never arrived for the appointment. That same day, Milburn had succumbed to caustic chemical exposure while cleaning a railroad tank car at the paper mill. He was 47.

Rod Milburn takes command of the Olympic 110-meter final in Munich. (Rich Clarkson Collection)

Endorsements were virtually non-existent, even for a gold medal winner like Milburn. At the time of his tragic death in 1997, Milburn was in the middle of a divorce and had moved into a homeless shelter in Baton Rouge. [115]

Willie Davenport

Track insiders criticized hurdler Willie Davenport for not training hard enough. As reported by *Sports Illustrated* in 1969, training was "a ritual Davenport religiously avoids."[119] Yet Davenport sustained one of the longest and most successful athletic careers of all time—five Olympic appearances, the gold-medal at Mexico City, bronze at Montreal, eight national championships, three world records, and five consecutive world No. 1 rankings from 1965 to 1969. Davenport remained one of the best hurdlers in the world for over a decade.

High hurdler Willie Davenport, gold medalist at the '68 Mexico City Games, poses on the track infield at Bowdoin. (Courtesy of Doug Morrell)

Self-described as a young thug with a terrible temper, Davenport's early years were inauspicious at the mostly white Howland High School in Warren, Ohio.[119] Fred Johnson, a teacher at Howland, had many confrontations with Davenport but understood his disquiet and was a positive influence on the future world champion. "…in Willie's case it was a guy not keeping up with the next one and just getting pushed around, ignored," said Johnson. "So he developed a plain sour attitude toward the whole world."[119] Bolstered by Johnson's support, Davenport went out for track his junior year and tried hurdling for the first time when his team needed extra points; Davenport won the race that day and a year later set the state record in the 120-yard high hurdles.[120]

Davenport enlisted in the Army after graduating from high school in 1961 and continued to hone his hurdling technique while deployed as a paratrooper in Mainz, Germany. In 1964, Davenport won the 110-meter hurdles at the Olympic Trials in Los Angeles, upsetting five-time national champion Hayes Jones. Davenport was among the favorites to win gold at the Tokyo Games, but he pulled a thigh muscle and did not advance to the finals. Davenport received an honorable discharge from the Army in 1965 then enrolled at Southern University where he earned five national titles in the 60-meter hurdles indoors, and three titles in the 110-meter hurdles outdoors.[121] Davenport was in peak form in 1968 when he avenged his loss in Tokyo by winning the 110-meter gold medal at Mexico City in an Olympic record 13.3. Davenport recalled battling his nerves before the start of the Olympic final: "When I walked to the starting line, I felt so weak that I didn't think I had the strength to take my sweat clothes off…but when that gun fired, in my very first step, I knew I had won the race."[120]

Between completing a bachelor's degree in physical education in 1969 and a master's in education in 1974, Davenport competed in the 1972 Olympic Trials where he placed second in the 110-meter hurdles and qualified for the Munich Games—his third Olympic appearance. Davenport qualified for the hurdle final in Munich, and he was in second place over the last hurdle before his form broke down and lost the bronze to teammate Tom Hill.

In 1975, Davenport underwent surgery for a knee injury and his doctor said he would walk with a limp and likely never compete again; Davenport disagreed: "…I was determined that not only would I run, but I would make the '76 Olympic Team."[120] Davenport regained his conditioning over the next several months and qualified for Montreal finishing second in the 110-meter hurdles at the Olympic Trials. At Montreal, Davenport capped his miraculous comeback by winning the bronze medal and was the top US finisher—at age 33.

Willie Davenport nicknamed "Breeze," looks askance as he clears the high hurdles in his first heat in Munich. (Press photo)

In an interview with Gus Weill of Louisiana Public Broadcasting in 1983, Willie Davenport, then 40, spoke confidently of his plans to qualify for a fifth summer Olympics at the Los Angeles Games. "I'll be there…I'm pushing for the gold," remarked Davenport.[120]

Davenport competed in his fifth Olympics as a member of the four-man US bobsled team at the 1980 winter Olympics at Lake Placid. Davenport, along with teammate Jeff Gadley, became the first African Americans to compete in the winter Olympics, and he was only the fourth American to compete in both the summer and winter games. The team placed 12th, but Davenport felt the US sleds were inferior: "It was like we were driving Model T's and the rest of the world was in Rolls Royces."[122] Davenport retired from competition shortly after injury ended his bid to compete at the Los Angeles Games in 1984.

Davenport served on the US Olympic Committee for 12 years and rose to rank of colonel in the Army National Guard. As chief of the Guard's Office of Sports Management, he traveled across the country connecting with, and inspiring, kids of all ages. The indefatigable Willie Davenport died of a heart attack in 2002, three months before retiring from the National Guard.

Ralph Mann

A native of Long Beach, California, Ralph Mann was the favorite to win the 400-meter hurdles at the Olympic Trials in 1972, and he did not disappoint. Mann won the final in an American Record of 48.4, two-tenths of a second ahead of Richard Bruggeman of the Ohio Track Club. At the Munich Games, Mann competed in the 400-meter hurdles final where he surged in the closing meters to pass David Hemery of Great Britain and claim the silver medal by one one-hundredth of a second. The winner, John Akii-Bua of Uganda, was only ranked 10th among the entrants but set an astonishing world record of 47.8, three-tenths of a second better than the record set at the Mexico City Games. Akii-Bua explained he had trained over hurdles with a 25-pound weighted jacket.[123]

Ralph Mann signals the start of an interval on the Bowdoin track. (Courtesy of Portland Public Library Special Collections & Archives)

While at Brigham Young University, Mann was the first in NCAA history to win three consecutive 440-yard hurdle championships (1969-1971). His performances included a world record 48.8 on a wet track in 1970. Upon smashing the previous record that had stood for 10 years, Mann commented "I don't know what I might have run if it hadn't rained."[124] Mann won gold at the Pan American Games in 1971 and was a four-time AAU national champion from 1969 to 1971, and in 1975. Mann was elected to the National Track and Field Hall of Fame in 2015.

After earning a Ph.D. in biomechanics from Washington State University in 1975, Mann became Associate Professor and Director of the Biomechanics Lab at the University of Kentucky. In 1982, he founded CompuSport, Inc., which specialized in biomechanical analysis and performance improvement for elite athletes, particularly sprinters and hurdlers. Dr. Mann was a pioneer in sports science and helped create the Elite Athlete Program that brought biomechanics and computer analysis to USA Track and Field.

400-meter hurdler Ralph Mann with an autograph seeker at Whittier Field. (Author's personal collection)

Ralph Mann out leans David Hemery of Great Britain to win the silver medal at the Munich Games. (Rich Clarkson Collection)

At his induction into the Carson High Athletic Hall of Fame at age 70, Dr. Mann commented, "The older I get, the better that medal looks. At that point I thought I was a failure, but you know a silver medal is pretty good now."[125]

Richard Bruggeman

Despite building a slight lead midway through the 400-meter hurdles at the '72 Olympic Trials, Richard Bruggeman had to settle for second place when Ralph Mann, the race favorite, charged into the lead. Both Mann and Bruggeman broke the American Record of 48.8, but it was Mann's time of 48.4 that would stand in the record book; Bruggeman ran 48.6. At the Munich Games, Bruggeman suffered severe shin splints a week before the competition. Despite efforts to tape his leg, he could not keep pace with the leaders and failed to advance from his qualifying heat. His two teammates competed in the finals, with Mann capturing silver and Jim Seymour narrowly missing bronze.

A native of Marion, Ohio, Bruggeman left his father's 1,800-acre corn and soybean farm when Ohio State University recruited him as a promising hurdler out of Elgin High. Under the mentorship of coach Bob Epskamp, Bruggeman became the Big Ten 440-yard hurdle champion in 1968, and he was an All-American in 1970 placing second in the indoor 600-yard run. Shortly after graduating in 1972, he won the AAU national championship in the 400-meter hurdles in 50.0. Bruggeman credits much of his success to Wayne Armburst who was at Ohio State for a Ph.D. in physics but studied track theory as a hobby. "Armburst improved my style, corrected some bad habits. I knew what to do to keep in physical shape, but I couldn't watch myself run," said Bruggeman.[126]

Richard Bruggeman in Maine, one month after winning the 400-meter hurdles at the AAU national championships at the University of Seattle. (Author's personal collection)

Bruggeman continued to compete after the Munich Olympics and was a member of the US National Track and Field Team that toured the People's Republic of China in 1975.[127] Bruggeman retired from competition in 1976 and began a career in real estate. In September 2018, he became a member of the Ohio State Hall of Fame during a celebration at half-time of the Ohio State-Rutgers football game.

Richard Bruggeman in his qualifying heat of the 400-meter hurdles in Munich. (Rich Clarkson Collection)

Bruggeman received the Marion County, Ohio, Walker Award for athletic achievement in 1972. In an interview with The Marion Star, *Bruggeman commented, "It was a great thrill and honor to be on the Olympic Team. I always wanted to wear the US colors. I think it's the dream of everyone who runs track."*[128]

Dave Roberts gets ready for a vaulting session at Whittier Field. (Author's personal collection)

Roberts had never been to Maine before the training camp and enjoyed the cool climate and rugged coast. "I loved it up there. I am sort of a 'nature freak,'" he admitted. Roberts recalled becoming good friends with Prefontaine, Jenner, and fellow vaulter Jan Johnson, and added: "You do not want to get in a ping-pong match with Bruce Jenner."

Dave Roberts

Raised in the hill country of Conroe, Texas, Dave Roberts was the state pole vault champion in 1969, then competed for Rice University from 1970 to 1973. While at Rice, he won three NCAA vault titles, and in the spring of his junior year he cleared 18-0 ¼ at the '72 AAU national meet to become one of only four vaulters in the world to break 18 feet. He was among the favorites at the Olympic Trials in 1972 and had high hopes for the Munich Games beyond. "This is nice," said Roberts after the AAU nationals, "but it's nothing like winning the Olympics."[129]

Roberts tied the Olympic record of 17-8 ½ at the Olympic Trials, but he could not match the powerful field of US vaulters that day and placed fourth—missing an Olympic team birth by one place. For the first time in history, three US vaulters, Bob Seagren, Steve Smith and Jan Johnson, cleared 18 feet; Seagren broke the world record clearing 18-5 ¾.[27] Smith became injured after the Trials and Roberts, the alternate, joined the training camp in Maine and competed in the pre-Olympic meets in Norway. Smith ultimately competed in Munich but did not advance past the qualifying round with a vault of 15-9.

After his disappointment at the Olympic Trials in 1972, Roberts was determined to take on the world's best vaulters at the Montreal Olympics. In 1975, Roberts was a first-year medical student at the University of Florida and joined the venerable Florida Track Club. That same year, he broke Bob Seagren's world record by clearing 18-6 ½ at the Florida Relays in Gainesville. Roberts dominated the US field at the Olympic Trials in 1976 by setting a new world record (18-8 ¼) on the way to becoming the top qualifier for the Montreal Games.

At the Monreal Games, Roberts was on script to win the Olympic pole vault title as he worked his way into a six-way tie for first in the final. Confident, and with a world record vault over 18-8 just a month earlier, Roberts opted to skip the next height (18-2 ½) and attempt 18-4 ½. The strategy looked golden as his competition failed at the lower height. But rain fell as Roberts began his attempts he too failed to clear the bar. Roberts held on to the bronze medal and faced criticism for his gamble. "I have no complaints," Roberts remarked. "I don't think it was a tactical mistake. I vaulted just the way I wanted to."[131] Roberts retired from competition shortly after Montreal and earned his M.D. in 1979. He continues to practice medicine as an emergency physician and assistant professor at the University of Florida College of Medicine.

Dave Roberts vaults at the Olympic Trials in Eugene, June 22, 1976. (Rich Clarkson Collection)

During Robert's first world record attempt at 18-8 ¾, his pole snapped, nearly breaking his hand and leaving it numb. With two attempts to go, Roberts borrowed a pole from Earl Bell and broke the record—a mark set earlier in the year by Bell. Bell ended up tied for second and remarked: "It's the vaulter who breaks the record, not the pole."[130]

US Long Jumper Randy Williams stretches on the runway at Whittier Field. (Courtesy of Portland Public Library Special Collections & Archives)

Randy Williams

At the long jump final in Munich, 19-year-old Randy Williams placed his teddy bear on the grass, stripped off his sweats and soared 27-0 ½ to win the gold medal on his first jump.[132] A gift from his girlfriend, William's teddy bear Roscoe became his lucky charm as 1972 unfolded with a string of winning jumps. But on the day of the long jump final in Munich, Williams had reason to doubt: "I ran about 30 minutes on the practice track outside the stadium. When I came in and started doing some stretching exercises, I heard something pop in my left leg." Williams knew he had to make his early jumps count, and with Roscoe watching on, he beat the field on his first attempt.[132] Williams became the youngest to win gold in the Olympic long jump and set a world junior record of 27-4 ¼ in the qualifying round that stood for 40 years.

Williams grew up in Fresno, California, and credits his mom for giving him permission to try the long jump after watching a track meet on the way home from school in 1966. In his first track season as a seventh grader, Williams jumped over 16 feet but failed to qualify for the West Coast Relays. "I went home and cried. I told Coach Lee I would come back the next year and win both, which I did. I jumped 19-4 in the long jump and 40-8 in the triple," recalled Williams.[133] During his senior year, Williams won the state championship in 26-3, a jump that would have set the national high school record but was wind aided.

Randy Williams (hooded sweatshirt) on the sidelines with US sprint team members John Smith (white shirt, center) and Vince Matthews (Nike shirt); Len Hilton runs in the foreground. (Courtesy of Portland Public Library Special Collections & Archives)

Williams enrolled in the University of Southern California in 1971, drawn by the success of Trojan jumping great Henry Hines, who had just set the school record of 26-8 ½ in the spring of 1971. With Hines as his training partner, Williams qualified for the US Olympic team by placing second at the '72 Olympic Trials by a scant ¾ inch behind Arnie Robinson who jumped 26-4 ¾. Robinson was ranked No. 1 in the world in 1971, but Williams topped the rankings in 1972 setting up a decade-long rivalry between the two California natives. Both long jumpers qualified for the '76 Games in Montreal, but this time it was Robinson who would win gold, with Williams the runner-up. Williams qualified for his third Olympics in 1980 but could not compete because of the US boycott of the Moscow Games. He retired from competition after failing to qualify for the Los Angeles Games in 1984, where he placed eighth in the Olympic Trials with a jump of 25-7 ½. In 2009, Williams was inducted into the National Track and Field Hall of Fame.

In early October 1972, organizers of the Fresno District Fair honored Williams and his girlfriend, Cookie Phillips. As reported by *The Fresno Bee*, "If time permits, Williams and Miss Phillips will occupy a box in the grandstand to watch the afternoon, and concluding, performance of championship rodeo,"[134] After five years in the marines and 22 years as a firefighter, Williams retired to coach—and raise cattle.[133]

Randy Williams' gold medal jump at the Munich Olympics. (Press photo)

Williams' mother, Idel, encouraged her son to pursue his dream of becoming an Olympic champion. "She's always givin' me things, my mother. And she never takes anything from me. Ever since I made the team I told myself, 'if you and Roscoe get lucky over there and win some kind of a medal, that's going to be mom's medal. '"[132]

Randy Williams, with his good luck bear Roscoe, in the stadium at the Munich Games. (Rich Clarkson Collection)

US Olympic long jumper Preston Carrington with a fan at Whittier Field. (Author's personal collection)

Carrington has his Adidas spikes in hand but a pair of early Nikes under foot. The new footwear company pushed hard to get Nikes on the feet of the distance squad and other Olympic team members before the Munich Games.

Preston Carrington

Preston Carrington was virtually unknown among the US long jumping elite, and he traveled to the Olympic Trials in 1972 with funds raised by donors in his college town of Wichita, Kansas.[135] Carrington considered his obscurity an advantage: "I was a little more relaxed than some of the others. I wasn't one of the ones they had picked to make it."[136] With Mexico City gold medalist Bob Beamon and former world best Ralph Boston sitting on the sidelines because of injuries, Carrington, the 20th-ranked jumper in the US, had an outside chance to make the Olympic team. After a modest opening jump of less than 24 feet, Carrington launched 26-0 ½ and took the lead after the qualifying round. In the finals he nailed his first jump at 26-4 which held up for the third and final qualifying spot at the Munich Games. In the preliminary round in Munich, Carrington landed what would be the second-best jump of the Games with a personal best 26-11 ½; but in the final, prior marks would not count. In the Olympic final, Carrington fouled twice then cleared 26-2 ½, to place fifth—less than 2 inches from the bronze medal.

While Carrington was little known on the national long jump scene, he was a star at Wichita State University. He started at guard in basketball and was an All-American in track, placing third in the NCAA long jump championships in 1970. By the time he graduated from Wichita State, Carrington had set school records in the high hurdles, long jump, triple jump and 100-yard dash; he also had the second-best high jump at 6-8 ¾.[137] In an interview with *The Wichita Beacon*, Coach Herm Wilson praised his jumper: "Preston is very versatile, 'Mr. Do-Everything'...Preston can go just as far in track and field as he has ambition to go."[137]

After Munich, Carrington continued his part-time coaching position at Wichita State, then signed-on to compete as a professional athlete with the ITA alongside Olympians Jim Ryun, Bob Seagren, Brian Oldfield, Lee Evans and Bob Beamon. After the inaugural ITA indoor season in 1973, Carrington earned $3,500; the top earner was 400-meter star Lee Evans who earned $13,500.[138] Carrington competed with the ITA through 1974 then retired from competition and began a lifelong career as a respiratory therapist.

Preston Carrington (left) with 110-meter hurdler Rod Milburn (right) under the pines at Whittier Field. (Author's personal collection)

Preston Carrington takes flight in the long jump at the Munich Games. (Rich Clarkson Collection)

Preston's coach at Wichita State, Herm Wilson, was trackside throughout the long jump competition in Munich. He watched as Preston sprung off the board in the finals and soared well over 27 feet. As Preston rose from the pit, an official raised his red flag—Carrington had fouled and lost his medal-contending jump. "He did a whale of a job, fifth best in the world," remarked Wilson. "He did a job of which he can be proud."[139]

US Olympic discus thrower Tim Vollmer with fans at Whittier Field. (Courtesy of Doug Morrell)

Tim Vollmer

Tim Vollmer was ranked among the top five US discus throwers from 1968 to 1973, climbing to No. 2 behind Jay Silvester in 1971. Vollmer won the AAU national title in 1971 with a throw of 208-4, and at the AAU championships in 1972 he threw 212-1, losing to Silvester by less than a foot. Even as a top contender to make the Olympic team, Vollmer struggled early in the '72 Trials, and it was not until the fifth round of throws that he moved up two places to finish third and lock in a trip to Munich.[27] Vollmer finished eighth in Munich, one notch better than his No. 9 world ranking with a mark of 60.24 meters (197-7 ½). Vollmer's teammate, 34-year-old Jay Silvester, won silver—his first medal in three Olympic appearances.

A native of Portland, Oregon, Vollmer excelled in the discus at Benson High School where he was the state champion in 1964 and 1965, and he was nationally ranked with a throw of 178-10 his senior year.[140] Vollmer competed for Oregon State University where he earned All-America honors as the runner-up in the NCAA nationals in 1968 and 1969. Vollmer joined the Army after graduating from Oregon State and competed for the Army track team into 1972; he then joined the New York Athletic Club, home to the top thrower in the world—Jay Silvester. Besides competing at the Munich Olympics, Vollmer's international experience included finishing runner-up at the Pan American Games in Cali, Columbia in 1971 and first at the US-Africa dual meet in Dakar, Senegal in 1973.[141]

US Olympic team qualifiers in the discus (left to right) Tim Vollmer, Jay Silvester and John Powell at Hayward Field, site of the '72 Trials. (Press photo)

One of Vollmer's last meets was an invitational to raise funds for restoration work at the University of Oregon's Hayward Field in Eugene. Vollmer was among 20 Olympians headlining the event held on June 8, 1974.[142] The historic Hayward Field stadium, the site of the Olympic Trials in 1972, 1976, 1980, 2008, 2012 and 2016, was razed to make way for a new facility completed in 2020.

'72 Olympian Fred Luke during a throwing session at Whittier Field. (Author's personal collection)

Luke was among the throwers in Maine who made the training camp organizers aware that the throwing area was not long enough, and adjustments were made. Luke faced the same problem four years later at a meet in Burnaby, British Columbia, where his throw over 280 feet hit a soccer net that event organizers neglected to move. "We just never thought anyone could throw that far," said a meet official.[143] *Luke's throw, which would have set a Canadian national record, was nullified because of the obstruction.*

Fred Luke

While Fred Luke trained with the Olympic team in Maine, fans in his hometown of Bellingham, Washington, celebrated the Munich-bound javelin thrower. They showed their appreciation by displaying, at the Whatcom Museum of History and Art, an "almost-life size" picture of him competing at the Olympic Trials.[144] The small coastal city proudly supported Luke who had risen from the sixth-ranked US thrower in 1971 to finish third at the Trials. Having won the AAU national championship two weeks earlier with a throw of 277-5, the University of Washington graduate was among the pre-Olympic Trials favorites. But even after moving into second after the preliminaries, he was under pressure. "Luke was pacing the infield like a caged lion about this time, knowing that his second-place standing could be knocked out by the other six United States finalists," reported *The Bellingham Herald*.[145] Luke erased all doubt with his final throw of 267-9, nearly eight feet farther than the fourth-place finisher.

Luke placed eighth at the Munich Games with a mark of 266-10 ½. US teammate Bill Schmidt, who finished behind Luke at the AAU championships, won the bronze medal with a throw of 276-11 ½. Even though it was the best one-two finish by the US in the javelin since 1952, Luke later revealed he had strained an abdominal muscle shortly after arriving in Europe for a series of tune-up meets.[146]

Luke set his sights on Montreal and redoubled his efforts to return to the Olympics in better form. His work paid off as he improved his personal best to 280-8 in winning his second AAU national championship in 1976, just two weeks before the Olympic Trials. But as the Trials unfolded, Luke was not himself, placing ninth in the qualifying round and barely making the finals with a throw of 246-11. He reached 263-8 in the finals and settled for fifth, ending his four-year journey for a second chance at an Olympic medal.

Luke stepped away from open competition after Montreal, but he continued to compete in masters track and field, including top age group finishes in world competition. After retiring from a longtime career as a welding engineer, Luke began coaching throwers at Archbishop Murray High School in 2006, then at Northwest University in 2019.

Fred Luke in 1975, upon his return from competition in China. (Press photo)

Luke was a heavy favorite coming into the '76 Olympic Trials in Eugene, Oregon, and his failure to qualify for the Montreal Games was confounding. In response to a string of sub-par performances at the Trials, one reporter commented: "…so it went in probably the most pressurized track meet in existence. There was a total of 120,000 spectators in track-mad Eugene and the final two days the tickets were $7 a copy."[147]

Olympic Sprint Coach Stan Wright with relay batons at Whittier Field. (Author's personal collection)

Coaching Legends

US POLE VAULTER JAN JOHNSON DESCRIBED THE OLYMPIC team leadership as a "Who's Who" of track coaches in America. The picks of the US Olympic Committee were Bill Bowerman as head coach, assisted by coaches Stan Wright (sprints), Hoover Wright (400 meters), Bill McClure (field events), Ted Haydon (distance) and Bruce McDonald (race walk). These six men shepherded the Olympic track and field team through the Maine training camp, pre-Olympic meets in Europe and the ultimate destination—the Munich Games.

The coaching team's role was to plan, organize, and unify the US team; the athletes would continue with their own coaches, or as was often the case, coach themselves. As described by Kenny Moore in his book, *Bowerman and the Men of Oregon*, Bowerman addressed the team on the opening day of the training camp in Maine: "We are absolutely honored to be here. We have been trying to keep things flexible, and our first job is to convince you magnificent stud horses that we want to help, and not just tell you what to do. Olympic coaches don't do much real coaching, certainly not until they're asked." Bowerman continued, "Do you know George Frenn? You'd get a hammer in your ear if you tried to tell him anything he didn't want to know."[148]

Head Olympic coach Bill Bowerman and his prodigy, Steve Prefontaine at Whittier Field. (Courtesy of Doug Morrell)

Bowerman was a master of team logistics and committed to the care and comfort of his athletes. Frustrated with the thick official Olympic racing singlets issued to the team, he had substitutes made from a lightweight knit material he found at a fabric store in Maine.[148]

Bill Bowerman

The USOC selected Bill Bowerman as the head track and field coach for the Munich Games in early 1972. The USOC recognized Bowerman's two-plus decades of impactful coaching at the University of Oregon, and his command of men and logistics while organizing the US Olympic Trials and training camp at Lake Tahoe in 1968. As a vocal advocate for athlete's rights, including compensation, Bowerman distanced himself from the powerful AAU and consideration for the role as head Olympic coach. Yet he proudly accepted the job he acknowledged as "the greatest honor that can come to a person in track and field."[149]

Bill Bowerman, Steve Prefontaine and Lee Evans watch decathlete Jeff Bannister over the hurdles at Whittier Field. (Author's personal collection)

Bowerman's footwear is a descendent of his invention that began in 1971 with urethane and a hot waffle iron. The inventor sought to create a shoe sole with better grip—the Nike waffle took hold and sales soared when released in late 1973.

The training camp in Maine was widely successful in offering a balance of training, relaxation, and engagement with track fans and the press. In Munich, however, Bowerman faced a barrage of crises that began with the threatened protest of Rhodesia's participation in the Games, the disqualification of two top US sprinters, and the deadly terror attack on September 5. Bowerman openly criticized the USOC and the handling of the Games by the German organizers. Just three days into the Olympics, Bowerman told the press: "You ask me if I'm happy, the answer is no. This is a lousy job. We're going to do all right, but it won't be fun."[150]

In the aftermath of the Munich Olympics, the decades-long coaching veteran was blunt in his assessment: "Worst experience in my total athletic career."[151] But Kenny Moore credited Bowerman with his leadership under intense pressure: "Bill's problem-solving abilities under fire, his bringing in the marines, his gifts for sizing up individuals and defending them against the bureaucracy, his putting the Olympic ideals into a few well-chosen words, all kept his Olympians safe and ushered a number through grief to the other side. …We would have been lost without him."[151]

Stan Wright

Stan Wright narrowly missed being selected as head coach of the US Olympic track and field team in Munich. The close vote that prevailed in favor of Bill Bowerman ignited controversy, as the convention had been to promote the assistant coach from the previous Olympics.[152] At the 1968 Mexico City Games, that coach was Stan Wright. In a memoir cowritten with Neil Amdur, Munich 400-meter champion Vince Matthews expressed his opinion unequivocally: "A black was not yet 'ready' to become a head coach in track and field, the glamor sport of all Olympic Games."[153]

A graduate of Springfield College, Wright began his career at Texas Southern University, where he coached from 1951 to 1967. His "Flying Tigers" drew national attention with performances at the Texas, Kansas and Drake relays, and Wright coached four Olympians, including Bill Hines, the Mexico City gold medalist and former world record holder in the 100-yard dash. Wright served on the USOC and The Athletics Congress, and he became the first black head coach of a US national team when he led the US in competition against Poland and the Soviet Union in 1966.[154] Two years later, he was the assistant coach at Mexico City where athletes under his care set five world records and won six gold medals.

Stan Wright (center) with assistant team manager Wally Ciochetti (right). (Courtesy of Portland Public Library Special Collections & Archives)

Wright immediately took responsibility for the schedule mix-up and disqualification of Eddie Hart and Rey Robinson—a selfless act that put him squarely in the crosshairs of an angry press corps and public opinion.

Wright was indispensable at the training camp in Maine. He managed sprint team workouts and helped quell discord between a few of the sprinters and Bowerman, whose management doctrine included a 10 o'clock curfew.[45] But on September 2, 1972, Wright accepted responsibility for the disqualification of 100-meter favorites Eddie Hart and Rey Robinson, and stood as the scapegoat for the sprinter's late arrival at their semifinal heats. While evidence later showed that US team management had not informed Wright of a schedule change, the press attacked him, and that same management was absent in his defense.[155]

Following Munich, Wright returned to coach at California State University, Sacramento, and remained devastated for well over a year, "I was just out of it," said Wright. "If I had been a quitter, I would have jumped off the Bay Bridge, taken poison or something."[156] Official inquiry into the schedule mix-up led to exoneration of Wright, and in 1993, he became a member of the National Track and Field Hall of Fame. Wright passed away five years later, at age 78.

Hoover Wright

Hoover Wright (no relation to Stan Wright) joined the Maine Olympic training camp as assistant coach of the 400-meter sprinters and hurdlers. He coached at Prairie View A&M University, and members of the Olympic sprint team questioned the skills of a coach not representing a powerhouse like UCLA or San Jose State.[157] Vince Matthews, however, had seen Wright's athletes perform at a high level and respected him as a coach. While preparing for the Munich Games, Matthews credited Wright for helping him run faster by relaxing: "I had been running with my fists in a ball. Not balled tight, but in a ball. Hoover told me to run with my hands open, just letting my wrists flap a little bit and to lift my knees for relaxation."[157] Matthews steadily improved, grew confident, and ultimately won the 400 meters in Munich.

Wright served as head coach of Prairie View A&M track and field from 1961 to his death in 2003 at age 74. During his tenure at Prairie View A&M, Wright guided his teams to three NAIA track championships and coached 400-meter specialist Fred Newhouse who won gold in the 1,600-meter relay and silver in the 400 meters at the Montreal Games. Besides the Munich Olympics, his international coaching experience included the 1971 US-Soviet Meet, the 1975 Pan American Games, and the 1981 World University Games in Bucharest.

In 2000, Wright was severely injured and four of his athletes were killed in a van accident while traveling to a track meet in Pine Bluff, Arkansas. Three weeks later, Wright's team defended its title at the Southwest Athletic Conference indoor track championship. "I'm very proud of them. We asked them to look forward and to step up even though part of our team died, and some got broken up like me," said Wright while recuperating at home. "My point of view to them was every time they get a chance to compete, they should give it their best because they don't know if a second or third chance will be available to them."[158]

Hoover Wright flanked by Vince Matthews (left) and Chuck Smith (right) at Whittier Field. (Courtesy of Portland Public Library Special Collections & Archives)

Bill McClure

Bill McClure was among the most experienced of the coaches who arrived in Maine in July 1972. Over the course of his 47-year career at Abilene Christian University, University of South Carolina and Louisiana State University, McClure coached 145 All-Americans and guided athletes to All-America honors in every track and field event.[159] His Abilene Christian teams won seven titles each in track and cross country, and McClure became a member of the Abilene Christian Sports Hall of Fame in 1991. Beyond his mentorship of countless athletes, McClure served as chair and secretary of the NCAA Men's and Women's Track and Field Rules Committee, was president of the US Track and Field Federation, and a member of the US Olympic Track and Field Committee. A pioneer of equal rights, McClure is credited with starting the women's track and field programs at the University of South Carolina and Louisiana State.

McClure rose before dawn each day to run at the track and prepare for a job that he loved. On his first day as coach at South Carolina in early 1972, he told his team "I know track isn't everything to everybody, but it is to me." [160] His passion and tireless commitment led to the transformation of the Gamecock track program into a regional powerhouse, and the town of Abilene, Texas, became much more than the hometown of golfing great, Charlie Coody.

Before the Munich Olympics, McClure was confident the US team would excel, but cautioned: "It's not that we're [regressing]…It's just that the world is catching up. The Germans offer great talent in the pole vault. Russia, Germany and France all have outstanding sprinters. We'll be good, but so will the competition."[160] McClure's analysis was not wrong—Soviet Valeriy Borzov won gold in the 100- and 200-meter sprints, East German Wolfgang Nordwig won the vault, and France's Guy Drut was runner-up in the 110-meter hurdles.

Bill McClure keeps a watchful eye from the track infield at Bowdoin. (Author's personal collection)

Doug Morrell handles a steaming lobster at the Olympic team gathering at Mere Point. (Courtesy of Doug Morrell)

The Lobster Bake

NEARLY TWO-DOZEN MEMBERS OF THE US TRACK & FIELD team arrived at Mere Point in Brunswick, Maine, for a traditional Maine lobster bake on a sunny and warm day in late July 1972. The training camp organizers had planned social events for the athletes and welcomed the offer by Bowdoin alumn and volunteer track official, Bob Morrell, to host the bake. A parade of volunteers shuttled the athletes seven miles from Brunswick to the Morrell's cottage where dozens of lobsters, clams, corn and potatoes roasted in a bed of seaweed. Bob Morrell's son Doug, 21 at the time, recalled driving his Volvo 240 with Steve Prefontaine in the passenger seat and three of the world's top sprinters in the back: Eddie Hart, Rey Robinson and Robert Taylor. "I couldn't believe it," remarked Morrell. "I had Pre and the two fastest men in the world in my car."

Ron Crowe, the Bowdoin College dining services director and owner of a catering enterprise, arranged the feast. Crowe recalled having baked chicken on the menu, but hardly anyone said "no" to the offer of Maine's most famous crustacean. Olympic vaulter Dave Roberts had never eaten lobster before and became hooked from the first bite; "I think I had eight of them," he recalled. That was one less than sprinter Eddie Hart, who proudly claimed to have eaten nine lobsters and hundreds of clams during his stay in Maine.[14]

A handful of the athletes and guests brave enough to plunge into the chilly bay went swimming and waterskiing. A boat driven by 15-year-old Bill Morrell, Doug's brother, pulled the skiers that included Steve Prefontaine, Frank Shorter, and Jack Bacheler. Nan Morrell, Doug's mother, asked Prefontaine if he was worried he might get hurt while waterskiing. He responded with a grin, "I'm here to have fun."

Steve Prefontaine waterskies on Maquoit Bay (Courtesy of Doug Morrell)

Members of the US Olympic team line up for the feast (right to left): Eddie Hart, Kenny Moore, Steve Prefontaine, Robert Taylor and Dave Roberts (Courtesy of Doug Morrell)

The lobster bake was one of several events planned for the Olympians during their stay in Maine. The outings included a trip to Old Orchard Beach, a team dinner at Estes Seafood, and a tour of the bay by sailboat. Several members of the sprint team watched the film, "A Clockwork Orange," sponsored by Bowdoin College, while Dave and Jan Wottle took in the musical "Oklahoma" that played at the Brunswick Music Theater.[14]

Above, newlyweds Dave Wottle (center) and Jan Wottle (far right) relax on the Mere Point waterfront. (Courtesy of Doug Morrell)

Wottle was unwavering about his decision to marry just four days before the training camp and to have his wife join him for a "honeymoon" in Maine. In Munich, he went one step further—In order for Jan and several other US team member spouses to gain access to the dorms in the Olympic Village, Wottle and his co-conspirators crafted false credentials from photos and various Olympic documents. Security guards granted the wives access as American gymnasts.[161]

Dave Wottle on the shore at Mere Point. (Courtesy of Dave Wottle).

Doug Morrell (left) and Olympians Jan Johnson and Steve Prefontaine chatting with host family guests. (Courtesy of Doug Morrell)

Olympic marathoner Kenny Moore described Johnson and Prefontaine as "inseparable."[162] The two roomed together at the training camp in Maine, having become good friends after connecting a year earlier at a meet in Bakersfield, California. Johnson, a native of Chicago Heights, Illinois, was the third qualifier in the pole vault at the Olympic Trials, clearing 18-0 ½. Steve Smith was runner-up, and Bob Seagren won the Trials with a world record 18-5 ¾. In Munich, Seagren and Johnson won silver and bronze, respectively, despite a last-minute decision by Olympic organizers to ban the late-model Cata-poles used by the Americans. Johnson won his medal on a pole borrowed from Bruce Jenner.[163]

Above, the athletes and family guests lounge at the dock while Olympic high jumper Ron Jourdan heads up the ramp. (Courtesy of Doug Morrell)

Ron Jourdan was second in the high jump at the Olympic Trials at 7-3. He was injured coming into his event at the Munich Games and missed qualifying for the finals by an inch. Nicknamed "Spider Jourdan" for his long arms and legs, Jourdan had a win streak of nine meets where he cleared 7-0 or higher as a senior at the University of Florida.[164]

"...May the Best Man Win," at Whittier Field Stadium. (Courtesy of Blaine Moore)

Afterward

THE MUNICH OLYMPICS WILL ALWAYS BE REMEMBERED for the terrorist attack on September 5 that took the lives of 11 Israeli athletes. The athletes and the world that watched were horrified, but the IOC pronounced the Games would continue in defiance of the terror and in deference to the sacrifice of the athletes and investment in the games. As the US track and field team contemplated a return to competition, Frank Shorter spoke with resolve: "We have to spread the word by our performance that barbarism only makes Olympians stronger. We have to say, 'This is as scared as I get. Now let's go run.'"[165]

The US men embraced Shorter's resolve and competed with courage to earn 19 Olympic medals: six gold, seven silver, and six bronze. Rod Milburn set a world record in the 110-meter hurdles, and the 400-meter relay team of Larry Black, Robert Taylor, Gerald Tinker and Eddie Hart also set a world mark. Other team members defied long odds to bring home Olympic medals such as Frank Shorter in the marathon, Randy Williams in the long jump, and Dwight Stones in the high jump. The US also persevered through controversies that threatened to unravel the team. Robert Taylor salvaged a silver medal in the 100-meters as co-world record holders Eddie Hart and Rey Robinson watched from the sidelines. Bob Seagren and Jan Johnson vaulted to silver and bronze on borrowed poles, and the US 400-meter relay team won gold to glean redemption after injury and disqualification decimated the heavily favored 1,600-meter relay team.

Despite the terror and controversy in Munich, the legendary trackmen of '72 have inspired a generation of athletes. They were among the last true amateurs of their sport, a time when the AAU banned endorsements and other compensation for athletes seeking to compete in the Olympics. They slept on floors and in the backseats of cars, and traveled to meets on skimpy pay from part-time jobs. They logged thousands of miles and practiced for hours with the sole purpose of being the best in their discipline and to compete on the ultimate world stage—the Olympic Games.

Frank Shorter, Steve Prefontaine, Willie Davenport and others from the Munich Olympic team campaigned for years to diminish the power of the AAU and prevailed with the Amateur Sports Act of 1978. The bill paved the way for compensation of athletes and helped the US keep pace with subsidized athletes from Eastern Bloc countries. It was bittersweet for athletes such as John Smith and Rod Milburn, who earned prize money in meets sponsored by the ITA but were later ruled ineligible to compete in the Montreal Games.

When the ITA abruptly folded in 1976 and athletes could regain amateur status, the US boycott of the Moscow Games derailed a return to the Olympics by Smith, Milburn and others.

While the Olympics at Rome were televised across America in 1960, it was not until 1972 that viewership swelled with improved programming. On September 2, 1972, about 30 million viewers tuned in as Dave Wottle clawed from last place to win gold in the 800 meters, and six days later they agonized as American mile icon Jim Ryun tangled with another runner and fell to the track in the 1,500. On the last day of the Games, a captivated nation cheered as Frank Shorter pulled away from the field and cruised to the first US marathon gold medal in 64 years.

With their achievements, the amateurs of 1972 were unwittingly responsible for helping launch a multi-billion-dollar industry—the "running boom." Leading the charge were distance icons like Frank Shorter, Steve Prefontaine and Jeff Galloway who rallied millions of Americans to embrace running on the roads and track by the end of the 1970s. As reported by *The Washington Post* in 1979, "Running has been hyped and heralded as the sport that requires nothing and no one. One running writer has called it the most democratic sport. You don't need a partner, a court, or even any skill."[166]

By the end of the 1970s, the New York Marathon field blossomed to 14,000 and participation of women in road racing more than doubled. The first women's Olympic marathon was held at the Los Angeles Games in 1984—an achievement made possible by advocates like Kathrine Switzer, the first woman to run the Boston Marathon and founder of the Avon road racing series for women. Joan Benoit Samuelson, a Maine native and graduate of Bowdoin College, was the champion of that inaugural marathon.

While the US remains dominant, the competition for talent among a variety of new sports and endurance events has impacted track and field. In the 2000s, men's track and field medal counts dipped from a high of 19 in Athens (2004) to 10 in Tokyo (2021). After failing to meet expectations in Tokyo, members of the US team expressed frustration with the lack of an Olympic training camp because of the Covid-19 pandemic.[167] The road to Paris in 2024 may be the perfect time to bring the training camp back to Whittier Field, and all that was good in Vacationland.

Bowdoin College's Whittier Field and Magee Samuelson Track, newly renovated in 2019. (Copyright Bowdoin College)

Olympic Decathlete Jeff Bannister during an interview with the *Portland Press Herald*. (Courtesy of Portland Public Library Special Collections & Archives)

References

1. Nason, J. (1972, July 18). 54 U.S. Olympians due at Bowdoin for Practice. *The Boston Globe* (p. 24).
2. Shulman, H. (1972, July 28). Glorious 10 Days at Bowdon Ends for Olympians and Fans. *Portland Press Herald* (p. 23).
3. BBC. On this day 1950-2005, 1972: Rhodesia out of Olympics. Retrieved from http://news.bbc.co.uk/onthisday/hi/dates/stories/august/22/newsid_3549000/3549444.stm
4. Moore, K. (1996, August 5). Munich's Message Last Week's Tragedy Stirred a 1972 Olympian to Realize Anew that, for the Athletes, the Games Must go On. *Sports Illustrated Vault*. Retrieved from https://vault.si.com/vault/1996/08/05/munichs-message-last-weeks-tragedy-stirred-1972-olympian-realize-anew-athletes-games-must-go.
5. Dew, R. (1972, July 31). Bowdoin 'Recovering' from Olympic Fever. *Boston Herald*.
6. Fallon, R. (1972, July 23). Olympic Trio Bares Souls. *Portland Press Herald* (pp. 2B-4B.)
7. Nason, J. (1972, September 6). Old Man, 83, Salvages Olympics: "Games Must go On." *The Boston Globe* (p. 49).
8. Eaton, D. (2016, July 15). Oklahoma Native just misses Medal at 1972 Olympics. *The Joplin Globe*. Retrieved from https://www.joplinglobe.com/sports/local_sports/oklahoma-native-just-misses-medal-at-1972- olympics/article_fdcae246-dbf2-59ad-9cd0-a6eec4694d37.html
9. Zarnowski, F. (updated 2008). History of the Decathlon at U.S. Olympic Trials. Retrieved from https://decathlonusa.typepad.com/deca/files/history_of_the_us_olympic_trials_repaired.pdf
10. Markazi, A. (2015, July 30). How Bruce Jenner became an Olympic Icon Exactly 39 Years Ago. *ESPN*. Retrieved from https://abcnews.go.com/Sports/bruce-jenner-olympic-icon-39-years-ago/story?id=32788658
11. Jenner, B. and Finch, P. (1977). *Decathlon Challenge* (p. 32). Prentice-Hall, Inc., Englewood Cliffs, NJ.
12. Caitlyn Jenner's Maine Connection (1996, April). *Portland Magazine*. Retrieved from https://www.portlandmonthly.com/portmag/2015/06/theflagwasstillthere/
13. Nason, J. (1972, September 1). Coach's Snafu Costs U.S. 2 Olympic Sprinters. *The Boston Globe* (p. 29).
14. Hart, E. and Newhouse, D. (2017). *Disqualified, Eddie Hart, Munich 1972, and the Voices of the Most Tragic of Olympics* (p. 167). The Kent State University Press.
15. Hart, E. and Newhouse, D. (2017). *Disqualified, Eddie Hart, Munich 1972, and the Voices of the Most Tragic of Olympics* (p. 13). The Kent State University Press.
16. Hart, E. and Newhouse, D. (2017). *Disqualified, Eddie Hart, Munich 1972, and the Voices of the Most Tragic of Olympics* (p. 2). The Kent State University Press.

17. Knapp. G. (2000, September 10). Eddie Hart Wins Gold for his Outlook. *SFGate.* Retrieved from https://www.sfgate.com/sports/knapp/article/Eddie-Hart-wins-gold-for-his-outlook-3051673.php

18. Hart, E. and Newhouse, D. (2017). *Disqualified, Eddie Hart, Munich 1972, and the Voices of the Most Tragic of Olympics* (p. 192). The Kent State University Press.

19. Central Florida Sports Hall of Fame (2010). Rey Robinson. Retrieved from https://www.centralfloridasports.com/local-sports/halls-of-fame/polk-county-sports-hall-of-fame/2010-hall-of-fame-inductees/rey-robinson-bio/

20. Hart, E. and Newhouse, D. (2017). *Disqualified, Eddie Hart, Munich 1972, and the Voices of the Most Tragic of Olympics* (p. 196). The Kent State University Press.

21. Murray, J. (1972, September 2). Russian Robot zips to Gold…They never had a Chance. *The Boston Globe* (p. 21).

22. The Associated Press (2007, November 15). Olympic Champion Sprinter Robert Taylor Dies. *TRIB Live.* Retrieved from https://archive.triblive.com/news/olympic-champion-sprinter-robert-taylor-dies/

23. Hart, E. and Newhouse, D. (2017). *Disqualified, Eddie Hart, Munich 1972, and the Voices of the Most Tragic of Olympics* (p. 16). The Kent State University Press.

24. Ghosts of the Orange Bowl: Nick Kotys (2009, August 9). Retrieved from http://miamisouthpaw.blogspot.com/2009/08/ghosts-of-orange-bowl-nick-kotys.html

25. Delgado, K. (2013, September). *Dreams of Gold script.* Retrieved from https:/www.stage32.com/sites/stage32.com/files/assets/screenplay/102095/screenplay_102095_1.pdf

26. Hart, E. and Newhouse, D. (2017). *Disqualified, Eddie Hart, Munich 1972, and the Voices of the Most Tragic of Olympics* (pp. 167-168). The Kent State University Press.

27. *Track & Field News* (1972). Olympic Trials Results, Eugene Oregon, June 29 to July 9. Retrieved from https://trackandfieldnews.com/wp-content/uploads/2018/03/1972.pdf

28. Nason, J. (1972, August 14). Jamaican Quarrie 200 Meter Choice. *The Boston Globe* (p. 22).

29. Henderson, J., editor (1972). *1972 Olympic Games* (p. 27). Runner's World Magazine, World Publications, Mountain View, CA.

30. Henderson, J., editor (1972). *1972 Olympic Games* (p. 54). Runner's World Magazine, World Publications, Mountain View, CA.

31. Robb, S. (1999, July 1). Black's Life Back on Track, *South Florida SunSentinal.* Retrieved from https://www.sun-sentinel.com/news/fl-xpm-1999-07-01-9907010129-story.html

32. Montville, L. (1992, December 21). A Man to Lean on. *Sports Illustrated Vault.* Retrieved from https://vault.si.com/vault/710901#&gid=ci0258c016600526ef&pid=710901---090---image

33. Anderson, C. (2009, October 30). Answering to a Higher Calling. *Herald-Tribune*. Retrieved from https://www.heraldtribune.com/news/20091030/answering-to-a-higher-calling

34. Boilers, Inc. (2016). Former Purdue Split End Larry Burton on College Hall Ballot. Retrieved from https://purdue.rivals.com/news/former-purdue-split-end-larry-burton-on-college-hall-ballot

35. Olympedia, Chuck Smith, Biographical Information. Retrieved from https://www.olympedia.org/athletes/79053

36. Nason, J. (1972, August 18). 400 Meters Looks Like a U.S. Party – As Usual. *The Boston Globe* (p. 28).

37. UCLA (2013, April 17). John Smith Profile – UCLA Official Athletic Site. Retrieved from https://uclabruins.com/news/2013/4/17/208187794.aspx

38. Ripton, R. (1985, April 11). Track Star Smith Ends his Running Odyssey: Bruin Great, Now Working on His Acting, Comes Back to UCLA to Coach. *Los Angeles Times*. Retrieved from https://www.latimes.com/archives/la-xpm-1985-04-11-we-12136-story.html

39. Jones, L. (2016, August 10). John Smith Continues Coaching Legacy in Rio. *Los Angeles Sentinel*. Retrieved from https://lasentinel.net/87214.html

40. Moore, K. (1993, July 5). Former Quarter-Mile Champ John Smith new Oversees other Sprinters in their Quest to Excel. *Sports Illustrated Vault*. Retrieved from https://vault.si.com/vault/1993/07/05/keeping-track-former-quarter-mile-champ-john-smith-now-oversees-other-sprinters-in-their-quest-to-excel

41. Matthews, V. and Amdur, N. (1974). *My Race be Won* (p. 35). Charterhouse, New York, NY.

42. Matthews, V. and Amdur, N. (1974). *My Race be Won* (p. 304). Charterhouse, New York, NY.

43. Layden, T. (2021, February 24). Remembering a Forgotten Protest: Vince Matthews, Wayne Collett and the 1972 Munich Olympics. *NBCSports* Retrieved from https://sports.nbcsports.com/2021/02/24/remembering-a-forgotten-protest-vince-matthews-wayne-collett-and-the-1972-munich-olympics/

44. McKnight, M. (2019, November 15). A Brush with Greatness: The Puma Shoe that Upended the 1968 Olympics. *Sports Illustrated*. Retrieved from https://www.si.com/track-and-field/2019/11/15/puma-shoe-upended-1968-olympics

45. Matthews, V. and Amdur, N. (1974). *My Race be Won* (p. 340). Charterhouse, New York, NY.

46. Zirin, D. (2004, April 9). Bringing the Black Freedom Struggle into Sports. *Counterpunch*. Retrieve from https://www.counterpunch.org/2004/04/09/bringing-the-black-freedom-struggle-into-sports/

47. Burns, R. (2015). Lee Evans Profile: 400m 20-Year World Record Holder to attend the 2015 Golden West Invitational's "Olympic Day" Celebration. Retrieved from https://www.pausatf.org/wp-content/uploads/2015/05/LeeEvansProfile.pdf

48. Amdur, N. (1972, April 4). Ailing Knees Threaten Wottle's Hopes. *The New York Times* (p. 30).

49. Nason, J. (1972, September 5). The Mad Hatter Speaks of Luck. *The Boston Globe* (p. 25).

50. Davis, P. (2011, November 10). Professor's Halloween Costume Sends an Inspiring Message. *The Daily Illini*. Retrieved from https://dailyillini.com/opinions/2011/11/10/professoraes-halloween-costume-sends-an-inspiring-message-2/

51. Schnittker, R. (2014, December 8). Running Legend Dave Wottle was really a Miler. *Bring Back the Mile, America's Distance*. Retrieved from https://bringbackthemile.com/news/detail/running_legend_dave_wottle_was_really_a_miler

52. Repository staff report (2016, August 16). OHSAA to Honor Olympic Gold Medalist Dave Wottle of Canton. CantonRep.com. Retrieved from https://www.cantonrep.com/article/20160316/SPORTS/160319505

53. Briggs, D. (2012, June 24). Memories Fresh of Day Wottle Shocked the World. *The Blade*. Retrieved from https://webcache.googleusercontent.com/search?q=cache:t3Vnvu5NEnAJ:https://www.toledoblade.com/sports/2012/06/24/Memories-fresh-of-day-Wottle-shocked-world/stories/201206240089+&cd=1&hl=en&ct=clnk&gl=us

54. Reid, R. (1974, July 1). Gently, with a Big Kick, Meet Mild-Mannered Claims Adjuster Rick Wohlhuter Who, Rest Assured, is the World's Speediest Half-Miler, *Sports Illustrated Vault*. Retrieved from https://vault.si.com/vault/1974/07/01/gently-with-a-big-kick

55. Putnam, P. (1976, February 16). Wohlhuter's Better Half, For the Man who is the World-Record Holder in the 880, the Easier Part of the Mile Comes First, as he Demonstrated last Week in Louisville, *Sports Illustrated Vault*. Retrieved from https://vault.si.com/vault/1976/02/16/wohlhuters-better-half

56. Garcia, M. (2000, October 1). Big Spikes to Fill, *Chicago Tribune*. Retrieved from https://webcache.googleusercontent.com/search?q=cache:AGjpRQbMo9MJ:https://www.chicagotribune.com/news/ct-xpm-2000-10-01-0010010090-story.html+&cd=5&hl=en&ct=clnk&gl=us

57. Olympedia. Rick Wohlhuter. Retrieved from https://www.olympedia.org/athletes/79208

58. Brown, D. (1992, July 24). Wheeler Covered Dulaney-to-Munich Course in a Hurry. *The Baltimore Sun*. Retrieved from https://webcache.googleusercontent.com/search?q=cache:b4u314-aMkoJ:https://www.baltimoresun.com/news/bs-xpm-1992-07-24-1992206191-story.html+&cd=5&hl=en&ct=clnk&gl=us

59. Olympedia. Bob Wheeler. Retrieved from http://www.olympedia.org/athletes/79183

60. U.S. Track & Field and Cross Country Coaches Association (2021, May 20). Brown Paced Tennessee to 1974 Team Title. Retrieved from http://www.ustfccca.org/ncaa-100/doug-brown-tennessee-ncaa-di-outdoor-track-field-championships-steeplechase-two-time-winner

61. Track & Field News (1976). Olympic Trials Results, Eugene Oregon, June 19 to June 27. Retrieved from https://trackandfieldnews.com/wp-content/uploads/2019/10/1976.pdf

62. Rohe Era Track and XC Association. Rohe Track Era (1962-1971), Chuck Rohe Coaching Tree, Doug Brown. Retrieved from http://www.rohetrackera.com/doug-brown.html

63. Nason, J. (1972, August 24). Prefontaine: Tough Cookie. *The Boston Globe.*

64. Special to the New York Times (1972, August 24). Prefontaine's Workouts Are So Good They Scare Him. *The New York Times* (p. 55).

65. Henderson, J., editor (1972). *1972 Olympic Games* (pp. 34-35). Runner's World Magazine, World Publications, Mountain View, CA.

66. Jordan, T. (1977). *Pre* (p. 59). Rodale Inc.

67. University of Oregon. Steve Prefontaine Bio & Pix. Retrieved from https://goducks.com/sports/2003/12/18/30594.aspx

68. Jordan, T. (1977). *Pre* (pp. 61-67). Rodale Inc.

69. Jordan, T. (1977). *Pre* (pp. 101-102). Rodale Inc.

70. Hollister, Geoff (2008). *Out of Nowhere* (pp. 85-87, 125). Meyer and Meyer Sport (UK) Ltd.

71. University of Houston Men's Track and Field (2000, July 5). Cougar Track & Field Great Leonard Hilton Passes Away After Long Fight with Cancer. Retrieved from https://uhcougars.com/news/2000/7/5/Cougar_Track_amp_Field_Great_Leonard_Hilton_Passes_Away_After_Long_Fight_with_Cancer

72. Track & Field News (2020). U.S. Rankings – Men's 1500/Mile. Retrieved from https://trackandfieldnews.com/wp-content/uploads/2020/01/05-m1500RankUS.pdf

73. Bakersfield.com (2016, September 14). BC's Memorial Stadium Host to many Memorable Moments. Retrieved from https://www.bakersfield.com/news/bcs-memorial-stadium-host-to-many-memorable-moments/article_be62a01b-d18c-5a0a-b499-6536cf11c9d7.html

74. Galloway, J. The Olympic Quest. Retrieved from https://www.jeffgalloway.com/2008/04/11/the-olympic-q-2/

75. Galloway, J. Narrative from 1972 by Jeff Galloway. Retrieved from: https://www.jackdogwelch.com/?p=29018

76. Froberg, T. (2015, September 12). Galloway to Share Running Expertise. *Post Crescent.* Retrieved from https://www.postcrescent.com/story/sports/2015/09/12/galloway-share-running-expertise/72179054/

77. Lowe, M. (2012, August 4). Beach to Beacon: Samuelson Chooses Her Running Mates. *Portland Press Herald.* Retrieved from https://www.pressherald.com/2012/08/04/picking-her-running-mates_2012-08-04/

78. Shorter, F. and Bloom, M. (1984). *Olympic Gold, A Runner's Life and Times* (p. 81). Houghton Mifflin Company, Boston.

79. Shorter, F. and Bloom, M. (1984). *Olympic Gold, A Runner's Life and Times* (p. 78). Houghton Mifflin Company, Boston.

80. Henderson, J., editor (1972). *1972 Olympic Games* (p. 46). Runner's World Magazine, World Publications, Mountain, CA.

81. Shorter, F. and Bloom, M. (1984). *Olympic Gold, A Runner's Life and Times* (p. 86). Houghton Mifflin Company, Boston.

82. Shorter, F. and Bloom, M. (1984). *Olympic Gold, A Runner's Life and Times* (p. 20). Houghton Mifflin Company, Boston.

83. Shorter, F. and Bloom, M. (1984). *Olympic Gold, A Runner's Life and Times* (p. 38). Houghton Mifflin Company, Boston.

84. Shorter, F. and Bloom, M. (1984). *Olympic Gold, A Runner's Life and Times* (p. 51). Houghton Mifflin Company, Boston.

85. Nason, J. (1972, August 25). Hill the Choice in Marathon. *The Boston Globe* (p. 50).

86. Joynce, G. (2008, August 25). Memories of a dirty Olympic Marathon. *ESPN Page 2*. Retrieved from http://www.espn.com/espn/page2/story?page=joyce/080822

87. Eggers, K. (2019, September 17). Moore Adds Hall of Fame to his Story. *Portland Tribune*. Retrieved from https://pamplinmedia.com/pt/12-sports/438563-349321-moore-adds-hall-of-fame-to-his-story

88. Moore, K. (2006). *Bowerman and the Men of Oregon: The Story of Oregon's Legendary Coach and Nike's Cofounder* (p. 273). Rodale Inc.

89. Schwartz, T. (2008). Intertwining Ovals. *The Magazine of the University of Oregon*. Retrieved from http://scholarsbank.uoregon.edu/xmlui/bitstream/1794/8258/1/OQ_Summer08.pdf.

90. Burfoot, A. (2012, November 2). Kenny Moore Received Hirsch Journalism Award. *Runner's World*. Retrieved from https://www.runnersworld.com/races-places/a20815306/kenny-moore-receives-hirsch-journalism-award/

91. Moore, K. (2006). *Bowerman and the Men of Oregon: The Story of Oregon's Legendary Coach and Nike's Cofounder* (p. 303). Rodale Inc.

92. Moore, K. (1995, December 4). The End of the World. *Sports Illustrated Vault*. Retrieved from https://vault.si.com/vault/1995/12/04/718001#&gid=ci0258bfb6000e26ef&pid=718001---cover-image

93. Goldstein, R. (2002, May 28). Mamo Wolde, Olympic Marathon Champion. *The New York Times*. Retrieved from https://www.nytimes.com/2002/05/28/nyregion/mamo-wolde-olympic-marathon-champion.html

94. Canby, V. (1982, February 5). 'Personal Best,' Olympic Love. *The New York Times*. Retrieved from https://www.nytimes.com/1982/02/05/movies/personal-best-olympic-love.html

95. Jasper, D. (2007, February 24). Following his Tracks, Bowerman Author Gives Tour of Eugene. *The Bulletin*. Retrieved from https://www.bendbulletin.com/localstate/following-his-tracks/article_6bd58c13-0270-5653-9af6-1f4b268b2a7a.html

96. Burfoot, A. (2012, November 2). Kenny Moore Received Hirsch Journalism Award. *Runner's World*. Retrieved from https://www.runnersworld.com/races-places/a20815306/kenny-moore-receives-hirsch-journalism-award/

97. *Sports Illustrated* Staff (1969, June 16). Tallest, Fastest and Buggiest. *SI Vault*. Retrieved from https://vault.si.com/vault/1969/06/16/tallest-fastest-and-buggiest

98. Shorter, F. and Bloom, M. (1984). *Olympic Gold, A Runner's Life and Times* (p. 56). Houghton Mifflin Company, Boston.

99. Shorter, F. and Bloom, M. (1984). *Olympic Gold, A Runner's Life and Times* (p. 64). Houghton Mifflin Company, Boston.

100. Shorter, F. and Bloom, M. (1984). *Olympic Gold, A Runner's Life and Times* (p. 67). Houghton Mifflin Company, Boston.

101. Nesbit, J. (2001, September 1). Distant Heroes, An Athlete's Search for a Graceful Exit. *Runner's World*. Retrieved from https://webcache.googleusercontent.com/search?q=cache:OhV2zHOikN0J:https://www.runnersworld.com/advanced/a20833903/distant-heroes/+&cd=26&hl=en&ct=clnk&gl=us

102. DeMeester, P. (2021, September 27). Celebrating the 50K and the Young Bronze Age 1965-1980. *Heal and Toe Online* (p. 6). Retrieved from http://www.marciadalmondo.com/admin/pdf/marcia_mondo/2809202182heelandtoe-2021-num52.pdf

103. DeMeester, P. (2020, November 10). You Don't have to be a Rocket Scientist to be a Successful Race Walker but it sure Helps (pp. 2-3). *Heel and Toe Online*. Retrieved from http://www.vrwc.org.au/tim-archive/articles/wo-goetz-klopfer.pdf

104. Wayne State University (2004, September 19). Wayne State Athletics: Goetz Heinrich Klopfer. Retrieved from https://wsuathletics.com/news/2004/9/19/091904aah_152.aspx

105. SI Staff (1963, June 24). Faces in the Crowd. *Sports Illustrated*. Retrieved from https://vault.si.com/vault/1963/06/24/faces-in-the-crowd

106. DeMeester, P. (2020, October 19). 55 Years of Race Walking: The Rich History of Tom Dooley. *Heel and Toe Online*. Retrieved from http://www.marciadalmondo.com/admin/pdf/marcia_mondo/19102020578heelandtoe-2021-num03.pdf

107. DeMeester, P. (2020, November 10). You Don't have to be a Rocket Scientist to be a Successful Race Walker but it sure Helps. *Heel and Toe Online* (p. 4). Retrieved from http://www.vrwc.org.au/tim-archive/articles/wo-goetz-klopfer.pdf

108. Brutocao, R. (2018, December 6). Interview with Tom Dooley on *The Mentors Radio Show*. Retrieved from https://thementorsradio.com/

109. Mortland, J. (1972, July). The Munich Prelude. *Ohio Racewalker*. Retrieved from https://racewalk.com/ORW/ORW%201972-07.pdf

110. Jeansonne, J. (1972, July 5). Long Islander Hoofs it to Olympics. *Newsday*, Nassau Edition (p. 87). Retrieved from https://www.newspapers.com/image/714742652/?terms=Steve%20Hayden&match=1

111. Mortland, J. (1974, March). Olympic Report. Ohio Racewalker. Retrieved from http://mastershistory.org/wp-content/uploads/2017/11/ORW-1974-03.pdf

112. Wilcox, M. (2021, August 6). Grueling Event at the Olympics Didn't Have a Women's Version, so They Got Rid of it Altogether. *The Daily Caller*. Retrieved from https://dailycaller.com/2021/08/06/paris-2024-olympics-tokyo-mens-race-walk-event-gender-parity/

113. Schmalz, D. (2016, January 21). Bill Weigle, The one-time Olympian Walker now devotes his Energy to Walking—and perserving—Fort Ord." *Monterey County Now*. Retreived from https://www.montereycountyweekly.com/people/face_to_face/bill-weigle/article_f09bca72-bfc1-11e5-a249-87c2022f6d83.html

114. Henderson, J., editor (1972). *1972 Olympic Games* (p. 52). Runner's World Magazine, World Publications, Mountain View, CA.

115. Cart, J. (1997, November 17). Life's Hurdles Tragic for Olympic Medalist. *Los Angeles Times*. Retrieved from https://www.latimes.com/archives/la-xpm-1997-nov-17-mn-54740-story.html

116. Dhillon, G. (2020, February 27). Rodney Milburn – The Olympian of Opelousas. *Kreol International Magazine*. Retrieved from https://kreolmagazine.com/culture/features/rodney-milburn-the-olympian-of-opelousas/#.YZ_CfL3MIp

117. Nason, J. (1972, August 17). Fate Owes Milburn a Hurdles Record. *The Boston Globe* (p. 56).

118. McGill, S. (2005). Rod Milburn: The Double-Armed Man. *Hurdles First*. Retrieved from https://hurdlesfirstbeta.com/free-articles/issues/rod-milburn-double-armed-man/

119. Myslenski, S. (1969, March 17). The Woes of Wee Willie Wisp. *Sports Illustrated Vault*. Retrieved from https://vault.si.com/vault/1969/03/17/the-woes-of-wee-willie-wisp

120. Weill, G. (1983, November 21). Interview with Willie Davenport for Louisiana Legend Series, *Louisiana Public Broadcasting*. Retrieved from https://americanarchive.org/catalog/cpb-aacip_17-12z35pgh

121. USATF Hall of Fame. Willie Davenport. Retrieved from http://legacy.usatf.org/HallOfFame/TF/showBio.asp?HOFIDs=39

122. Lewis, T. (1998, February 6). Tough Sledding. *Times-Picayune* (p. D1).

123. Henderson, J., editor (1972). *1972 Olympic Games* (p. 53). Runner's World Magazine, World Publications, Mountain View, CA.

124. U.S. Track & Field and Cross Country Coaches Association (2020, July 25). BYU's Mann Set World Record in 440 Hurdles. Retrieved from https://www.ustfccca.org/ncaa-100/ralph-mann-byu-440-hurdles-world-record-1970-ncaa-outdoor-championships.

125. 2019 Inaugural Carson Colts Athletic Hall of Fame (2019, November 27). Retrieved from https://www.youtube.com/watch?v=KA3VC2QyWcU\

126. Burick, S. (1972, August 29). Ohio Ex-Farmboy Near Goal as Olympics Hurdles Winner. *Dayton Daily News* (p. 14).

127. United Press International. (1975, May 28). U.S. Track Team Ends China Tour. *The New York Times*. Retrieved from https://www.nytimes.com/1975/05/29/archives/us-track-team-ends-china-tour.html

128. Short, J. (1973, February 15). Dick Bruggeman Captures 1972 Walker Award. *The Marion Star* (p. 22).

129. Associated Press (1972, June 19). Dave Roberts Vaults 18 Feet; Fredericks Sets National Record. *The Mercury* (p. 30).

130. Putnam, P. (1976, July 5). Flying Start towards the Olympics. *Sports Illustrated Vault*. Retrieved from https://vault.si.com/vault/1976/07/05/flying-start-toward-the-olympics

131. Associated Press (1976, July 27). Gold Bouncing in U.S. Basketball Team's Direction. *The Central New Jersey Home News* (p. 10).

132. Nason, J. (19872, September 10). U.S. One Jump Away from Gold Medal Shutout, *The Boston Globe* (p. 94).

133. Fresno Athletic Hall of Fame. Olympian Inductees, Randy Williams. Retrieved from https://www.fresnoahof.org/olympian-details.php?id=332

134. Kidder, K. (1972, October 6). Fair Salutes Olympic Star. *The Fresno Bee* (p. 1).

135. Associated Press (1972, June 30). Derby Helping Olympic Drive. *The Wichita Beacon* (p. 7A).

136. Hanley, R. (1972, July 11). Being Unknown Fine with Former Shocker. *The Wichita Beacon* (p. 9).

137. Mullen, D. (1971, March 25). Youngsters Spike WSU Track Team as Season Starts. *The Wichita Beacon* (p. 1C).

138. Mullen, D. (1973, June 19). Mulling about Sports. *The Wichita Beacon* (p. 3B).

139. Mullen, D. (1972, September 21). Mulling about Sports. *The Wichita Beacon* (p. 3C).

140. Portland Interscholastic League Hall of Fame, Cyber Museum. Tim Vollmer. Retrieved from https://pilhalloffame.org/cybermuseum/benson/tim-vollmer/

141. Associated Press (1973, August 6). Africa Shows Track Potential in Losing to U.S. *Daily News* (p. 62).

142. Candland, S. (1974, June 5). Local Tracksters Enter UO's Hayward Field Meet. *The World, Coos Bay, Ore* (p. 17).

143. Associated Press (1976, May 3). Soccer Net Costs Fred Luke Record. *The Bellingham Herald* (p. 11).

144. Associated Press (1972, August 10). Fred Luke Faces Three Warmup Javelin Tests in Europe before Olympic Games. *The Bellingham Herald* (p. 4).

145. Carver, J. (1972, July 3). Fred Luke Third in Javelin Finals. *The Bellingham Herald.* (p. 7).

146. Associated Press (1972, September 4). Luke Finishes 8th in Javelin. *The Bellingham Herald* (p. 7).

147. Farris, B. (1976, July 4). Olympic Trials: Not Best, but Fairest Way. *The Fresno Bee* (p. H1).

148. Moore, K. (2006). *Bowerman and the Men of Oregon: The Story of Oregon's Legendary Coach and Nike's Cofounder* (pp. 281-283). Rodale Inc.

149. Moore, K. (2006). *Bowerman and the Men of Oregon: The Story of Oregon's Legendary Coach and Nike's Cofounder* (p. 254). Rodale Inc.

150. Associated Press (1972, August 30.) Bowerman Fires Salvos All Around at the Games. *New York Times* (p. 28). Retrieved from https://www.nytimes.com/1972/08/30/archives/bowerman-fires-salvos-all-around-at-the-games.html

151. Moore, K. (2006). *Bowerman and the Men of Oregon: The Story of Oregon's Legendary Coach and Nike's Cofounder* (p. 304). Rodale Inc.

152. Hart, E. and Newhouse, D. (2017). *Disqualified, Eddie Hart, Munich 1972, and the Voices of the Most Tragic of Olympics* (p. 180). The Kent State University Press.

153. Matthews, V. and Amdur, N. (1974). *My Race be Won* (p. 303). Charterhouse, New York, New York.

154. U.S. Track & Field and Cross Country Coaches Association, Stan Wright, Coaches Hall of Fame, Class of 1998. Retrieved from http://www.ustfccca.org/awards/stan-wright-ustfccca-class-of-1998

155. Hart, E. and Newhouse, D. (2017). *Disqualified, Eddie Hart, Munich 1972, and the Voices of the Most Tragic of Olympics* (p. 180). The Kent State University Press.

156. Harvey, R. (1993, November 29). The Fall Guy: At Least Stan Wright Gets to the hall of Frame on Time. *Los Angeles Times.* Retrieved from https://www.latimes.com/archives/la-xpm-1993-11-29-sp-62198-story.html

157. Matthews, V. and Amdur, N. (1974). *My Race be Won* (pp. 296-298). Charterhouse, New York, New York.

158. Lutz, M. (2000, March 1). Track Team finds Resolve, Wins Conference Championship. *The Monitor* (p. 7C).

159. LSU Athletics (2019, July 11). Former Track & Field Coach Mill McClure Dies, 86. Retrieved from https://lsusports.net/news/2019/07/11/1474478-2/

160. Helms, H. (1972, February 20). A Runner in the Night. *The State* (pp. 3C, 9C).

161. United Press International (1972, September 23). U.S. Olympians Smuggled Wives into Village. *El Paso Herald-Post* (p. 7).

162. Moore, K. (2006). *Bowerman and the Men of Oregon: The Story of Oregon's Legendary Coach and Nike's Cofounder* (p. 282). Rodale Inc.

163. Ryan, K. (2011, April 7). Olympic Medalist Jan Johnson has not Forgotten his Chicago Heights Roots. Patch. Retrieved from https://patch.com/illinois/chicagoheights/olympic-medalist-jan-johnson-hasnt-forgotten-his-chicf8bd826540

164. Associated Press (2014, January 3). Ronnie Lee Jourdan (1947-2014) *Northeast Mississippi Daily Journal.*

165. Moore, K. (2006). *Bowerman and the Men of Oregon: The Story of Oregon's Legendary Coach and Nike's Cofounder* (p. 299). Rodale Inc.

166. Leavy, J. and Okie, S. (1979, September 30). The Runner: Phenomenon of the '70s, *The Washington Post.* Retrieved from https://www.washingtonpost.com/archive/sports/1979/09/30/the-runner-phenomenon-of-the-70s/ba9e2a3d-a353-4f89-a3ba-b8c38b354034/

167. Niesen, J. (2021, August 8). The once-great US men's track team failed to win a solo gold in Tokyo. Why? *The Guardian.* Retrieved from https://www.theguardian.com/sport/2021/aug/08/usa-mens-track-team-medals-olympics-tokyo

Made in the USA
Columbia, SC
17 December 2024

49826341R00072